RAIL TRAILS
along the
GREENBRIER RIVER

D1430492

Rail Trails
along the
Greenbrier River

by Jim Hudson

Quarrier Press
Charleston, WV 25301

Quarrier Press
Charleston, WV

Copyright 1998 by Jim Hudson

Second Edition

10 9 8 7 6 5 4 3 2

Printed in the United States of America

Library of Congress Control Number: 98-66202
ISBN: 1-891852-00-0

Book, cover and map design:
Mark Phillips/Marketing+Design Group

Distributed by:
Pictorial Histories Distribution
1125 Central Avenue
Charleston, WV 25302
www.wvbookco.com

TABLE OF CONTENTS

Acknowledgments

This book is a revised edition of my previous guides to rail trails in the Greenbrier River Valley. Although extensive work has been done to the trail to correct damage caused by past floods, some recent flood damage has still not been corrected. This book includes those changes which have been made to the trail, and additional minor revisions.

Mr. William Price McNeel, author of *The Durbin Route* and *The Greenbrier River Trail: Through the Eyes of History* was helpful in providing additional information on the railroad and suggesting changes and corrections to the earlier text.

This book is dedicated to the Baboon Bike Club: Bill Robinson, Bob Delauter, Tammy Delauter, and Wanda Guthrie who have helped in many ways during the field trips and writing of all three editions.

Photo Credits

All photographs by Jim Hudson except page 28, by Frank Proud and page 32, by Marty Weirick, both of West Virginia Rails-To-Trails Council.

PART ONE
Introduction
* * *

CHAPTER ONE
Introduction to this Guide

This guide covers two rail trails in the Greenbrier River Valley: the West Fork Trail and the Greenbrier River Trail. The West Fork Trail (TR 312) is primarily suited for hiking and horseback riding. The Greenbrier River Trail is suitable for hiking, biking, horseback riding, and cross country skiing. Although this guide is primarily oriented around the Greenbrier River, the West Fork Trail roughly parallels four rivers at different points: Shavers Fork, Dry Fork, the West Fork of Glady Fork (all tributaries of the Cheat River), and the West Fork of the Greenbrier River.

Some explanatory remarks about directions and terms used in this book are in order. The West Fork Trail is described as beginning at Glady and going to Greenbrier Junction, and then going from Glady to Durbin. The West Fork Trail is hook shaped, with the northernmost point not actually at the end of the trail. However, to simplify matters, I call the Shavers Fork end of the trail "the north end" and the Durbin end "the south end."

The Greenbrier River Trail roughly parallels the main stem of the Greenbrier River, which flows north to south. However, the Chesapeake & Ohio Railroad traditionally referred to their tracks that ran along the Greenbrier River as running east and west. Some old guidebooks refer to such sites along the trail as "the west portal of Sharps Tunnel," or "the east piling of the Watoga Bridge." For the C & O on this line, east is

upriver and west is downriver. To be consistent with the West Fork Trail, I have used the term "north" for the Cass end of the trail, and "south" for the North Caldwell end.

Unless the context clearly indicates otherwise, the terms "left" and "right" with reference to the trails refer to one standing and facing in a southerly direction. In other words, as you face Durbin (south) on the West Fork Trail, and North Caldwell (south) on the Greenbrier River Trail.

The mileage figures given in this book are of two types. A mileage figure having two digits after the decimal point, (i.e., 4.25) indicates that the mileage figure came from a railroad or geological survey. (In referring to railroad stations, the mileage is measured to the original depot or flag stop, not the present town or road crossing. Because some of the old railroad stops consisted of relatively temporary sheds and structures which are now gone, these figures may not be exactly precise.) A mileage figure in this book with one digit after the decimal point, (i.e., 4.2) indicates that the mileage figure is an estimate taken from maps, geological survey reports, field measurements, or other sources. Elevation figures given are estimates, derived from railroad surveys, geological surveys, topography maps, or other resources.

The Western Maryland mileage figures begin in Baltimore. The West Fork Trail is described as beginning in Glady at milepost 299.2, and extending "north" to Greenbrier Junction at about milepost 295 and "south" to Durbin at about milepost 321. The C & O mileage figures begin where the Durbin Route joined the mainline at Whitcomb. The Greenbrier River Trail description starts in Cass at milepost 80.68, and ends at North Caldwell in a small park at milepost 3.3.

I have used several abbreviations in this guide that may or may not be standard. These are:

CR County Route
WV West Virginia State Highway
US Federal Highway
FR United States Forest Service Road
TR Designated Hiking Trail.

A major trail in the Greenbrier River Valley which this book refers to repeatedly is the Allegheny Trail (TR 701). It runs from the West Virginia/Pennsylvania border near Morgantown, to the West Virginia/Virginia border near Lake Sherwood. It is not shown on all current topographic maps. The Allegheny Trail crosses the West Fork Trail at Glady and again at Durbin. It joins the Greenbrier River Trail at Cass and accompanies it to Sitlington, where it turns east along Sitlington Road (CR 12) for about 1 mile. Several trails connect the Greenbrier River Trail and/or the West Fork Trail with the Allegheny Trail. A number of good circuit hikes are possible using combinations of two or three of the trails. For such hikes, you'll need some basic map skills and *The Hiking Guide to The Allegheny Trail*, published by the West Virginia Scenic Trails Association. The Allegheny Trail was designed and constructed for pedestrians only; mountain bikes or horses should not be ridden on it. A substantial number of other trails also connect with the Greenbrier River Trail. These trails vary in length and difficulty, and can be combined for different adventures.

It is beyond the scope of this book to give a comprehensive list of all the trails in the Greenbrier River Valley. However, I have noted several additional trails that intersect with the two rail trails. Many trails, not in this book, are equal in beauty, ease of access, and degree of difficulty as those I have included. Information on additional trails is available through other guidebooks, some of which are listed in the bibliography.

After spending a short time hiking, you'll quickly realize you can get enjoyment from many different aspects of a hike in the wild. You may find that you use your camera and guidebooks as much as your boots. The geology, flora, and fauna are constant distractions. You will end up wanting to identify at least some of the different species that you see.

Now, how long will it take you to hike these trails? I don't know. Because few of us hike or ride without stopping, and everyone goes at a different pace, it is impossible to give even an estimated time it will take to cover any particular trail. Often, two trail sections of similar length and difficulty will take radically different amounts of time to hike, for a multitude of reasons. As hinted at above, once you start stopping to identify every spring wildflower, any specific reference to an expected completion time goes out the window. To prevent influencing anyone's pace or leisurely enjoyment of a trail, I have refrained from including my hiking times. A general guideline for hiking times is: allow a half hour for each mile of hiking. On trails with substantial elevation gradients, (not the two rail trails featured in this book) you should add an additional half hour for every 1000 feet of change in elevation. Instead of a time estimate, I have only given the length of each trail or trail section in miles, as taken from maps or field estimates.

While traveling along the Greenbrier or West Fork Trails, you may notice markings which indicate the intersection of another trail with the rail trail. These intersecting trails are marked by a system of colored blazes: orange diamonds, yellow squares, red circles or some other combination of color and shape. A single blaze marks the trail. A double blaze, usually one above the other, indicates a change in direction. Some trails are marked with colored plastic blazes cut from detergent bottles. These plastic blazes rarely fade and are easy to see. Since they are held in place with a single nail or staple, they do little damage to trees. I hope more trails are marked with these recycled materials in the future. However, sometimes blazes disappear due to weather, vandals, fallen trees, or other causes. Therefore, always keep track of your whereabouts on a map and don't rely solely on the blazes. You must also recognize the truth of the geographer's maxim: "The map is not the terrain." Sometimes there are no blazes and the map is simply wrong. In those cases, use your own judgment and hope for the best.

I'd also recommend reviewing a couple of the many how-to books on hiking. They usually cover equipment, the health benefits of hiking, and the techniques for hiking with minimal impact on the environment. My favorite is Colin Fletcher's *The Complete Walker III*, but many other excellent guides are available. I suggest you read at least one before setting off on a long hike.

CHAPTER TWO
Introduction to the Region

The Appalachian Mountains were originally elevated during the Permian Era, over 280 million years ago. Through erosion by wind, water and ice — and subsequent uplifting — this area has been shaped into its current surface topography. The surface rocks consist of Permian, Pennsylvanian, and Mississippian sandstone, shale, clay, conglomerate, coal, and limestone. The Allegheny Front is the dividing line between the Appalachian Plateau and the Valley and Ridge Province. The Allegheny Front runs along the top of the series of mountains between Shavers Mountain and Droop Mountain. It is also to the west of the Greenbrier River, the West Fork Trail, and the Greenbrier River Trail.

While hiking these trails, you'll see a multitude of native plants which are indigenous to these sections of West Virginia. Many other species have been brought into the region by early settlers, or inadvertently spread by travelers. Again, I would suggest carrying a guidebook on plants and wildflowers while you hike. It can be fun and rewarding to identify new plants.

Many species of wild animals were found in the region at one time. The last Eastern Buffalo or Wood Bison (*Bison athabascae*) recorded in West Virginia was killed near Valley Head in Randolph County in 1825. The last recorded elk or wapiti (*Cervus elaphus*) killed in West Virginia also met its fate in Randolph County, in 1843. In 1936, panther (*Felis couguar*) tracks were found in Pocahontas County. Several people have reported seeing panthers since 1936, but nobody has provided definitive tracks, pictures, or other proof. The last known wolf killed in West Virginia also met its fate in Randolph County, in 1905. According to farmers from the Lewisburg area, coyotes are moving into the region. It is unknown whether these are true coyotes (*Canis latrans*) or some mixture of wild dog, coyote, and wolf.

Weather conditions in the trails' regions are usually mild, except for the winter months. Under normal conditions hiking is possible most of the year. Randolph County has an annual precipitation of 52.8 inches and an average July high temperature of 81 degrees (Fahrenheit). Pocahontas County has an annual precipitation of 43.8 inches and an average July high of 85 degrees. Greenbrier County has an annual precipitation of 41.9 inches and an average July high of 86 degrees. In general, the lower elevations have a lower annual precipitation and warmer temperatures. Heavy snow along some parts of the two trails may make long winter hikes difficult. As you would expect, however, that is the best time for cross country skiing along the Greenbrier River Trail. Randolph County averages between 60 and 120 inches of snow each year. Pocahontas County averages between 50 and 120 inches. Greenbrier County averages only 25 to 60 inches.

Because the elevation varies greatly in these regions, you may experience dramatic weather changes on these rail trails. The weather averages given above shouldn't be relied on too closely, especially if you plan to be out on the trails for an extended period. For example, in March I have gone from shirt sleeve weather along the Greenbrier River to being stuck in snow on the top of Buckeye Mountain, all in the space of an hour. I have also seen snow flurries in early April along the West Fork Trail. For this reason, try to bring appropriate clothing, in case a surprising West Virginia storm system comes in and defies the latest forecast.

The peak times for vibrant fall foliage are: late September for Pocahontas County, early October for

Randolph County, and late October for Greenbrier County. Lower elevations have their peak color later than higher ones. To see spectacular colors throughout the region, time your visit for early October.

For interested fishermen, the Greenbrier River is renowned for its small mouth bass. Other fish in these rivers include large mouth bass, sunfish, rock bass, catfish, walleye, pike, muskies and trout, all of which are stocked in the cooler portions of the rivers.

Following I have named some reminders of potential hazards to be aware of while enjoying our rail trails. First, many of these areas are used extensively by hunters. Be aware of the appropriate hunting seasons and wear blaze orange if there is any question in your mind about the possible presence of hunters. Hunting is not allowed on Sundays, making Sunday a good day to hike! From time to time the legislature changes the seasons slightly, so check to confirm the following hunting seasons in West Virginia:

1) **Small Game Season:** First Saturday in October through December 31;
2) **Deer Season (rifle):** Monday before Thanksgiving for two weeks;
3) **Spring Gobbler Season:** Third week in April through the third week in May.

Second, watch out for rattlesnakes and copperheads, both of which are found in West Virginia. Snakes will avoid you if given the opportunity. However, watch where you put your hands and feet, especially when on sun-warmed rocks. Other wild animals will also usually avoid humans.

Third, keep an eye out for dogs. Many of the dogs that live in the area are not accustomed to hikers and bikers — some even seem to detest us. Few of the area dogs are caged or tied up. Those that are confined will still announce to the world that you're there. Even when you are on a trail, they perceive you as an intruder in their world. I have been bitten by a dog while riding along the Greenbrier River Trail north of Marlinton. Use care when passing through a dog's territory.

Finally, be conscious of private property. Although the trails in this book run through or adjacent to the Monongahela National Forest, they sometimes parallel private property. The right-of-way for rail trails is usually only one hundred feet wide. Where the trail is in the National Forest or a state park, you are permitted to wander further from the trail in some areas. However, in many places the trail is a good distance away from other public lands, and private property surrounds the trail. **WHEN IN DOUBT STAY ON THE TRAIL!** The many cabins, camps, and private homes along the trails were not built to provide camp sites, firewood, rest rooms, river access, or water for trail users.

CHAPTER THREE
What to Carry on an Outing

A few items should be carried on every outing, no matter how short. The exact items are a matter of personal preference, but they do fall into predictable categories. The following list of recommended items is in no particular order.

SUN PROTECTION

The bare skin showing through my hair makes wearing some type of hat or cap a necessity. I also carry a pair of sunglasses and a small bottle of sun block, all year around.

RAIN AND WIND PROTECTION

Try to carry some type of lightweight rain gear. If you keep it light enough, you'll always carry it with you. A jacket in the closet won't keep you dry in the woods. As stated earlier, sudden storms can drastically, and unexpectedly, alter the temperature and conditions.

MAP OR GUIDEBOOK

Get a good guidebook or map of the area and study it before setting out. *(For additional information on maps, see Chapter Four of this book.)*

BANDANNAS

I always carry two. In my experience, they've served as a pot holder, nose wiper, eyeglass cleaner, washcloth, towel, expedient hat, and a dozen other uses. Their versatility is limited only by your imagination. I recently found a bandanna with a trail map of Blackwater Falls State Park printed on it. I'm still looking for one with a checkerboard printed on it.

TOILET PAPER

Few public toilets exist along these trails. It is imperative that all trail users practice appropriate sanitary procedures. Even in civilization, you may find toilet facilities missing important supplies. I carry pocket tissues for this and a number of other uses. A small bar of soap is also handy.

FIRST AID KIT

No two people agree on what is necessary in a first aid kit. A few bandages, a piece of moleskin for incipient blisters, a small container of insect repellent, sunscreen, a couple of aspirin, and some sinus tablets are always in mine. Develop your own kit based on what you need, and know how to use. Keep it small enough so that you'll always carry it!

LIGHT NYLON CORD

An acceptable substitute for shoe laces, expedient lanyards, belts, and one thousand and one other uses. Ten to twenty feet has always been enough for me.

WATER CONTAINER

Water containers come in a multitude of shapes and sizes. I try to have at least six ounces of water available for every mile I intend to hike. Carry all you expect to need, or carry some means to purify it. Raw sewage flows into some of the streams from towns, isolated houses, and camps along the trails. Other streams traverse cow pastures, or have other agricultural activities taking place along their banks. What appears to be pure spring water may be bubbling up from a nearby pasture. *NO FREE FLOWING OR STANDING WATER IN WEST VIRGINIA IS SAFE TO DRINK AS IT IS.*

FOOD

Every hiker, even those out for just an hour, should carry

some kind of snack. An hour hike could become a two hour one, by choice or by accident. Granola, beef jerky, peanut butter crackers or fresh fruit will do on short hikes. You might try the new "breakfast bars" and athletic "power bars." Both are nutritious, but try them out before you go — some are better than others.

COMPASS

I carry a compass when in the woods. But, in all honesty, I seldom look at it except to orient myself to my maps. It remains tucked away — a security blanket to fall back on if need be. Forget using a watch and the sun to tell direction. It is easy to be off by as much as 30 degrees with this method.

WATCH

Some people may hike to forget the pressures of time and having to watch the clock. However, to avoid getting stranded at sunset, carry a watch and keep an eye on it. Also remember to allot more time for the second half of your hike than for the first.

FIRE STARTERS

Anyone who hikes should carry a few "strike-anywhere" matches in a waterproof match safe. I also carry a needle with a short length of thread, a safety pin, and a couple of birthday candles. Even if you don't plan on cooking or being out overnight, you should carry some type of fire starter that you know how to use. You may need a fire for emergency warmth, light, cooking, or to signal for help. An acceptable backup to matches is an inexpensive butane lighter.

SIGNALING DEVICES

Whistles are carried by wilderness travelers to announce their presence to wild animals or to summon help in emergencies. Yelling will work, but you can blow a whistle long after your vocal cords have given out from the strain of yelling.

PEN AND PAPER

I carry these to make notes about the trail, sketch maps, flowers, plants — and generally just to jot down thoughts I might forget in my old age. Pen and paper obviously are optional, but you might be surprised at what you'll be inspired to write down while out in the wilderness.

CHANGE

More than once I have thirstily come out of the woods, found a soft drink machine, and had no change! Once I needed to phone for a ride because of a crushed front bike wheel. But I couldn't, because my change was locked in my car, 50 miles away. Now I carry a couple of dollars in quarters taped to the inside of my first aid kit and in the tool pouch on my bike. I try to remember to replace them after I use them.

FLASHLIGHT

Anything from a cheap plastic disposable penlight to a heavy D-cell flashlight will serve the purpose. I carry a small one-cell "AAA" flashlight clipped onto my key ring. Sometimes I replace it with a larger two-cell "AA" one that fits into a belt holster. I am much more apt to carry one of these small lights than I am a big one. Flashlights have come in handy on various occasions.

KNIFE

From a little penknife for slicing Vienna Sausages to a giant fixed-blade bowie for splitting wood, everyone has their own preference in this department. I always carry a Leatherman® tool. Bill Robinson prefers the Swiss Army knife. I was thankful he had it on a cold, icy hike we once made in early March. We desperately needed staffs to cross icy stretches of trail. Without the saw on Bill's Swiss Army knife to cut the staffs, we probably would have slid into the river and gotten a chilling bath. I recently purchased the new Leatherman® Supertool with a saw because of this experience.

TOOLS
Bikers should carry appropriate tools to deal with minor hassles along the trail, such as repairing tubes, adjusting cables, or aligning handlebars. Also, make sure your air pump functions with the type of valve on your tires.

CARRYING ALL THIS STUFF
Most of the items I have listed will fit in your pockets if you wear a multi-pocketed vest or jacket. However, many people prefer to carry a pack. One option is the familiar "fanny pack." A popular alternative is a small backpack or day pack, which gets the load off your hips and onto your shoulders. A backpack also gives you the freedom to carry extra items. You probably want to base your "pack" choice on the length of your hike.

A COMPANION
The right companion can triple the pleasure of a day in the outdoors, not to mention increasing your safety. Of course, the wrong companion can be a major disappointment. Typically, the best companion is one of about your own level of ability and experience. However, be patient with a beginner who shows potential. Discuss your hiking experience and expectations. If you enjoy each other's company, and can recognize each other's limitations, it should be a good pairing. My friend Bill Robinson is an excellent companion for me. We don't insist on continuing when one is tired or time is running out. As bikers our motto is "Not to proud to push." Again, it's always best to take a buddy, especially on new

trails. If you must go out alone, let someone know where and when you are going, and that you will contact them upon your return.

CHAPTER FOUR
Maps and Additional Information

Maps come in many varieties. West Virginia, like other states, distributes free highway maps at rest stops, state police detachments, and other locations throughout the state. These maps show the major highways in the state and not much else. The current highway map is not as complete as older versions. Even so, it is better than many commercial maps that lump West Virginia with Virginia, Maryland and Delaware, and show little detail.

Much better for locating access points to trails and other remote locations are the General Highway County Maps – 1989. They come in two sizes. The smaller "Type B" size map is 11" by 18", and has a scale of two miles to one inch. The different counties are covered by different numbers of sheets. However, you can't buy just one sheet. You have to buy the entire county. Type B has always been adequate for my needs. The larger "Type A" map is 18" by 36", and has a scale of one mile to one inch. This size costs twice as much as the Type B and is harder to handle while traveling. A bound set of Type B or Type A maps covering all fifty-five counties is available. To get the county maps, write to the West Virginia Department of Transportation. (*For this address, see Appendix I.*) For the base price, plus shipping and handling, you will receive your maps within one to four weeks. If you can't wait, the Department of Transportation sells these maps, and others, over the counter on the eighth floor of the Highways Building (Building Five) at the State Capitol.

Better than the highway maps are topographical maps. These are commonly available in two sizes, 1:100,000 (30 by 60 minute) and 1:24,000 (7.5 by 7.5

minute). For hiking the West Fork and Greenbrier River trails, either size of the appropriate topos will also cover many areas you won't need. I photocopy the sections of the map that I'll need for a trip and carry the copies. I make notes on the copies and keep them in my files for future planning. This way, I still have the original untouched maps.

The 1:100,000 map covers a larger area than the 1:24,000 and it comes folded up for carrying. The larger size is more convenient for bikers who cover large stretches of trail between map reading sessions. However, it is a metric map and each contour interval is 50 meters. This 50 meter (160 feet) gap can mean a lot of up and down that goes unreported on the map.

I have carried both sizes of topo maps while hiking, biking, and canoeing along these rail trails. I have used them infrequently in the field, and virtually never on the Greenbrier River Trail. When canoeing, you follow the river. When hiking or biking, you'll find that both trails are broad and well-defined. This guide and the mileposts are adequate to identify your location along the Greenbrier River Trail. However, along the West Fork Trail, which has no mileposts, a topo map can be handy. If you decide to hike some of the many trails that cross the rail trails, get the appropriate topo maps and carry them. Once away from the river, the trails are not well marked and it is easy to get turned around.

Anyone ordering topographical maps should also request the free pamphlet (MAP-X1B) which explains the markings on them. While I don't carry this small brochure with me, I do review it frequently at home. Another handy free publication (MAP-X1A) is the index map for 7.5 minute topo maps. Topo maps are available in some outdoor shops, or can be ordered from the West

Virginia Geological and Economic Survey, or the United States Geological Survey. (*For the last two addresses, see Appendix I.*)

Recently a company named DeLorme began publishing computer generated topographical maps of West Virginia in a single atlas called the *West Virginia Atlas & Gazetteer*. Copies are available in bookstores statewide. Forty-four 1:150,000 scale maps cover the entire state and some adjoining areas in surrounding states. The maps are adequate for access to the rail trails covered in this guide and general planning, but the small scale covers too large an area for use in hiking other, less obvious trails. Too many important details are simply not included.

If you purchase this atlas be sure to read the introduction to all the sections before you depend on the information provided. I studied the description of the West Fork Trail several times before I realized that the distance given was round trip and not one way. Other distances, marked with an asterisk, are given as one way. This publication also states that the West Fork Trail passes the High Falls of Cheat River and Camp Allegheny. In actuality, High Falls is a few miles from the West Fork Trail. Camp Allegheny (the Civil War Camp, not the one at North Caldwell) is not on the trail, but is eight miles as the crow flies southeast of Durbin.

The trails in this book run through or adjacent to the Monongahela National Forest. The Forest Service has published a Forest Recreation Map at 1/4 inch to the mile. This folding map covers the entire forest, and includes most roads and trails, topographic contours (100 foot intervals), and many local points of interest. This is the map I usually carry. These maps are available at the Monongahela National Forest Headquarters.

Recently I purchased a new folding map from the Forest Service without examining it first. They now have a folding road map of the National Forest at 1/2 inch to the mile. While it lacks the topographic contours of the Forest Recreation Map, the increased detail in other features makes it worthwhile for planning.

The Forest Service provides a great deal of literature on the recreation areas and points of interest within the forest itself. It is worth checking with the Forest Service before setting off on a trip. These maps and additional literature on the forest and individual recreation areas are available from any of the National Forest offices in West Virginia. (*For addresses, see Appendix I.*)

The Greenbrier River Hike, Bike, & Ski Trail Inc. and the West Virginia park system offer one page maps of the Greenbrier River Trail. Sometimes these maps conflict with each other, and this guide, in minor details. However, they are adequate for the Greenbrier River Trail and its major access points.

Information on the Allegheny Trail (TR 701), and other trails, is available from the West Virginia Scenic Trails Association. (*See Appendix I for address.*)

A number of hotels and motels are scattered nearby, up and down the Greenbrier Trail. The West Fork Trail can only claim hotel space in Durbin. Some addresses are included in Appendix I. A few facilities in the area are not right on the trail but are oriented towards mountain biking and deserve special mention.

Elk River Touring Center, in Slatyfork, Pocahontas County, is one of the oldest facilities in the state specifically set up for mountain biking. Operated by Gil and Mary Willis, the Center rents, sells, and repairs bikes. Bike rentals include helmets and racks. The Elk River Touring Center operates out of the Willis' Inn at Slatyfork, having a full restaurant and bar, as well as cottages for rent. Also available for rent are in-line skates, tents, sleeping bags, and fishing gear. Elk River Touring offers two to six day guided bike tours of the area. It is also expanding its fly fishing services.

Snowshoe Mountain Biking Center offers mountain biking on designated trails on resort property when skiing isn't possible. A Snowshoe Trail Pass is required. They also offer a full range of sales, rental, and service of mountain bikes. Guided tours are available for single day, or multi-day tours of area inns and bed and breakfast's. Tennis courts, swimming, hot tubs, saunas, exercise centers, horseback riding, and gift shops are also available at Snowshoe.

Silver Creek Resort, just ten uphill miles from Cass, offers access to a variety of trails. Silver Creek offers bike rental, and guide service. Trail maps and general information are available at the front desk.

PART TWO
The West Fork Trail
* * *
CHAPTER FIVE
An Overview of the Trail

On August 1, 1903, the Coal and Iron Railway was completed. It was originally owned by Senator Henry G. Davis, and ran from Elkins to Durbin. At Durbin, it connected with the C & O Route along the main stem and the East Fork of the Greenbrier River. On November 1, 1905, Senator Davis sold it to the Western Maryland Railway Company. Its 46.38 miles of main line track and 5.77 miles of siding were initially used for hauling lumber out of the Cheat Mountain area and the upper Greenbrier River Valley. After the decline in the timber industry in the 1920's, the railway began hauling coal from the Cheat Mountain and Point Mountain coal fields. It later became part of the CSX Transportation network.

As major changes swung the market from timber to coal, the section of track between Greenbrier Junction and Durbin saw less and less traffic. Eventually this 28 mile section of track was abandoned. In 1986 it was taken over by the United States Forest Service and became the West Fork Trail (TR 312).

This rail trail follows the east bank of the Shavers Fork branch of the Cheat River from Cheat Junction northward. It skirts the town of Bemis by a half mile — Bemis is northeast and 300 feet below the trail — and turns eastward to the towns of Glady and Glady Fork. It turns south up the West Fork of Glady Fork to the Pocahontas County line and the divide between the Cheat watershed and the Greenbrier watershed. It follows the West Fork of the Greenbrier south to

Durbin. The elevation ranges from about 2,600 feet along Shavers Fork to 3,147 feet at the divide between the Cheat and Greenbrier watersheds.

Between the end of the West Fork Trail in Durbin and the Greenbrier River Trail lie 15 miles of right of way that are not currently used. Cass Scenic Railroad used to transport newly obtained rolling stock over this connection. This track has sat idle for a number of years. Recently a locomotive has begun running over two miles of this track. It should be expanded to four miles in the future. The West Virginia Rails To Trails Council has reached an agreement with the owner of the right of way. This agreement grants access to a four foot wide trail which parallels this stretch of track. By the turn of the century, there should be an uninterrupted trail for 120 miles from North Caldwell to Glady! The Greenbrier River Trail and the West Fork Trail will then be part of the second longest rail trail in the country. I suggest anyone interested in making this happen contact the West Virginia Rails to Trails Council, at (304) 722-6558.

Bikers wishing to travel both existing rail trails can use a network of County Routes as the connecting links. At Durbin, cross the old iron bridge and follow CR 250/13 (Old 250) uphill for about .3 mile to CR 250/11 (Grant Vandevender Road). Turn left and follow this road about .7 mile to CR 1 (Back Mountain Road). Turn left and follow Back Mountain Road about 11 miles to Cass. This route has spectacular scenery and allows for broad vistas of the surrounding terrain. On the down side, it is a very hilly 12 miles.

Hikers can use this same network of roads, or can continue to Cass on the Allegheny Trail. This section of the Allegheny Trail covers 20 miles of rugged and

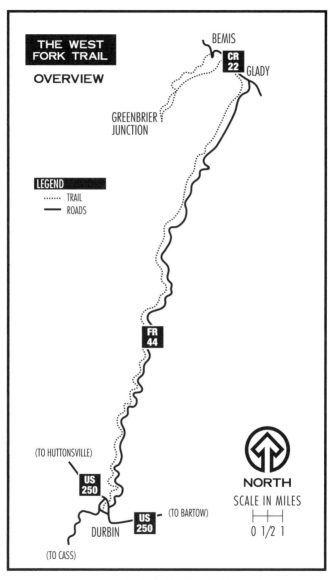

THE WEST
FORK TRAIL

OVERVIEW

BEMIS

CR
22

GLADY

GREENBRIER
JUNCTION

LEGEND
.... TRAIL
——— ROADS

FR
44

(TO HUTTONSVILLE)

US
250

US
250

(TO BARTOW)

DURBIN

(TO CASS)

NORTH

SCALE IN MILES

0 1/2 1

relatively isolated country. The Allegheny Trail follows the Greenbrier River Trail from Cass to Sitlington.

Scenery along the West Fork Trail varies from good to excellent. The more spectacular scenery on the trail appears as you move further away from Glady and Durbin. Other than the railroad bed and FR 44, there are few signs of civilization along the trail.

Like most rail trails, the West Fork Trail itself is obvious. There is little or no chance of losing the trail. The rails and ties have been removed, and a large portion of the graded surface consists of very loose cinders. The trail is suitable for a leisurely stroll, day hikes, overnight backpacking, cross country skiing, and horseback riding. Biking on the trail is best near Durbin, because the other sections have too soft a trail surface for easy riding.

Unlike the Greenbrier River Trail, the West Fork Trail does not have any mileposts or other signs along the route. It would be nice if small signs could be installed to identify the location of the named stations and the summit of the divide between the Cheat and Greenbrier watersheds.

The original trestles over the streams are still in place. So far, no effort has been made to cover the trestles with full decks. The open ties are acceptable for hikers, bikers, and skiers, but equestrians will have to ford the shallow streams. At periods of high water this may be dangerous. Motorized travel is prohibited along the West Fork Trail, and there are frequent gates along the trail to prevent it.

The West Fork Trail is owned by the Forest Service and passes through Monongahela National Forest for most of its length. However, it also passes through and beside private property, especially around Glady. Acceptable camp sites are numerous, but as always, be certain you are not on private property.

If you are traveling the trail during the warmer months, think about bringing your swimsuit or fishing gear. You'll find a number of deep pools which can ease sore muscles and rinse away the day's accumulation of sweat. There is also excellent fishing in all of the streams along the trail.

You may see canoes or kayaks anywhere along the 15 mile stretch from Wildell to Durbin. The best and most popular rapids are just above Durbin. Some people put in along Little River, take it down to the West Fork, and then travel south to Durbin. These streams are fast-paced, and suitable for accompanied beginners or intermediate paddlers. Several points along FR 44 allow access to the river. It is unlikely to see paddlers in the Cheat River while along the trail. Any you see will be experts, or idiots. Both would be worth watching.

Chapter Six
Glady to Greenbrier Junction

MILEPOST

299.20   Glady
298.8   Tunnel #2 Summit
296.7   Cheat Junction
296.80   Morribell
295.9   Red Roaring Run
295.6   Greenbrier Junction
293.5   Bemis

The northern trailhead is at Glady. The only public institution at Glady is the Glady Store. It has served as the post office since 1886, and now also sells food, soft drinks, candy, and basic medicines. The north end of FR 44 is about .5 mile east of the Glady Store along CR 22.

The section from Glady to Greenbrier Junction is difficult to bike in some places due to washed out areas and fallen rock. Hikers also have to watch their step in these areas. Although motorized vehicles are not allowed along the trail, apparently motorized four-wheelers frequent it. New trails have been created by these infernal internal combustion machines to circumvent the blocked sections.

From the Glady station you can travel about .25 mile northwest along the trail to the mouth of "Tunnel #2." ("Tunnel #1" is located 13 miles north of Bemis at milepost 280 along track that is still in use.) It is possible to travel through this quarter-mile tunnel, but it is not recommended — by the Forest Service or the author. Mounds of dirt have been placed at the mouths of the tunnel to discourage entry. Near the southern end of the tunnel is the old Western Maryland Railway Quarry. The green or bluish-gray Stoney Gap Sandstone from

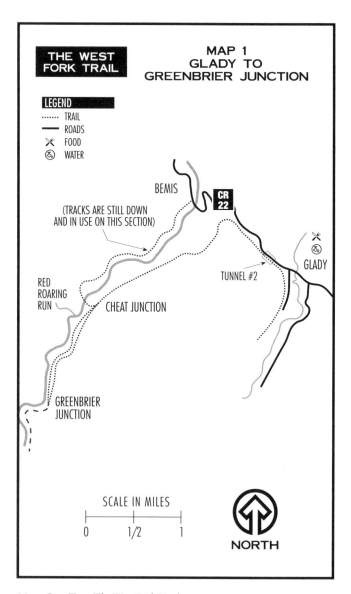

THE WEST
FORK TRAIL

MAP 1
GLADY TO
GREENBRIER JUNCTION

LEGEND
.... TRAIL
——— ROADS
✕ FOOD
🚰 WATER

BEMIS

CR
22

(TRACKS ARE STILL DOWN
AND IN USE ON THIS SECTION)

GLADY

TUNNEL #2

RED
ROARING
RUN

CHEAT JUNCTION

GREENBRIER
JUNCTION

SCALE IN MILES

0   1/2   1

NORTH

the quarry was used to line the tunnel. Over the years the annual cycle of freezing and thawing has crumbled the tunnel's lining. Anyone foolish enough to enter will contend with the potential hazard of falling and fallen rock, as well as extreme moisture. Sometimes over a foot of water collects inside the tunnel.

I recommend bypassing Tunnel #2 by following CR 22 west toward Bemis. About .7 mile from the Glady Store are five railroad ties set as posts separating the road from the trail. From here the trail cuts through a spur of Shavers Mountain and turns up Shavers Fork. Just after this noticeable turn in the trail, you can see the town of Bemis approximately .5 mile to the northeast, lying 300 feet lower in elevation than the trail.

Once the trail approaches Shavers Fork, you can look across the river and see the Western Maryland (now CSX) tracks that ascend Cheat Mountain from Bemis to Spruce, and west to Webster Springs. The trail here runs through "Mauch Chunk Shales," an ancient surface of shale and sandstone, where you can occasionally find marine fossils.

Published sources differ about what exactly constitutes the end of this trail. Some say it ends at Cheat Junction; others say it ends at Greenbrier Junction. One source says it ends at Cheat Junction, but includes a map showing it extending on to Greenbrier Junction. The Forest Service map indicates it stops about halfway between the two, opposite the mouth of Red Roaring Run.

Actually, the trail has two ends along Shavers Fork. About 1.7 miles from the five posts there is a "Y" in the trail. The right hand route turns downhill, crosses the tracks and river, and ends at Elk River Junction. The left hand route continues another 1.3 miles to Greenbrier Junction where it ends at the tracks.

About 1.4 miles beyond Greenbrier Junction are the High Falls of the Cheat and High Falls Trail (TR 345). This 5 mile trail crosses Shavers Mountain and connects with the Allegheny Trail on top of the mountain. It connects with the West Fork Trail and FR 44 on the east side of the mountain. It is easy to find the Falls from the end of the West Fork Trail. Just follow the Western Maryland right-of-way upriver to the horseshoe bend.

Chapter Seven
Glady to Durbin

MILEPOST

299.20 Glady
302.0   Beulah
302.7   Summit Cut
305.80 Wildell
308.7   Gertrude
310.60 May
311.1   Benchmark at northeast corner of the concrete
        abutment to trestle.
313.90 Burner
314.0   Benchmark at west end of south stone
        abutment on trestle over Little River.
316.10 Braucher
319.6   Olive
319.6   Benchmark at trestle over Mountain Lick Creek
        280 ft. east of Olive.
321.80 Durbin

From Glady, the West Fork Trail climbs up the West Fork of Glady Fork to the Pocahontas County line, and to the divide between the Cheat watershed and the Greenbrier watershed. It roughly parallels the West Fork of the Greenbrier River and FR 44 south to Durbin.

At one time the R. Chaffey Railroad connected to the Durbin Branch of the Western Maryland Railroad at Glady. The Chaffey railroad was originally owned by the Glady Manufacturing Company. The company's sawmill could cut 20,000 board feet a day. Richard Chaffey purchased the railroad in 1925. At that time it consisted of 14 miles of 42-inch gauge track. The sawmill and the railroad were removed by about 1931, when the timber supply was exhausted. It appears that CR 22 east of Glady follows the route of this railroad.

The West Fork Trail crosses the Allegheny Trail at Glady. This stretch of the Allegheny Trail is also known as the North-South Trail (TR 688), the Shavers Mountain Trail (TR 332), and/or the Randolph County Bicentennial Trail. For the next 18 miles, the Allegheny Trail climbs over 1,200 feet to the top of Shavers Mountain, where it finally reaches Gaudineer Scenic Area. From the Scenic Area, the Allegheny Trail roughly follows US 250 to Durbin and the south end of the West Fork Trail.

About 3.5 miles from the Glady Store, the West Fork Trail crosses the High Falls of Cheat Trail (TR 345). A gate, but no sign, marks this crossing. The Allegheny Trail is about 1 mile to the west along TR 345. FR 44 is about .5 mile to the east. The other end of the High Falls Trail crosses the Western Maryland Railroad right-of-way between Bemis and Spruce, a few miles past the end of the West Fork Trail. These three trails can be combined to form interesting loops for overnight backpacking trips.

The easiest access point to the trail in Glady is across from the National Forest Warden's house along CR 27, the road beside the Glady Store. Several additional access points exist along FR 44 and at the iron bridge in Durbin. The south end of FR 44 is a short distance up Highland Street across US 250/WV 92 from the iron bridge.

The trail surface from Glady heading south is extremely soft. Even fat tire bicycles tend to bog down in the loose cinders which make up most of the trail surface. Your normal riding speed will be cut in half, so plan accordingly for this section of the trail. As you approach Durbin, you will discover two narrow lanes

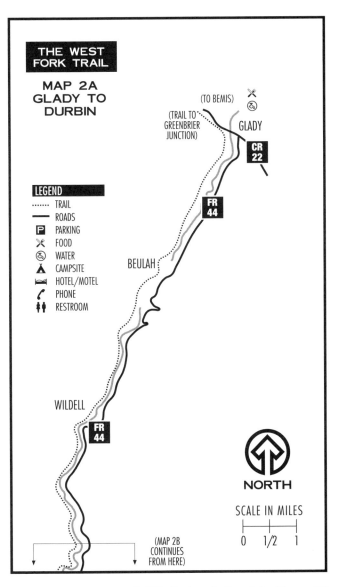

THE WEST
FORK TRAIL

MAP 2A
GLADY TO
DURBIN

(TO BEMIS)

(TRAIL TO
GREENBRIER
JUNCTION)

GLADY

CR
22

LEGEND
.... TRAIL
———— ROADS
P   PARKING
✕   FOOD
♿   WATER
▲   CAMPSITE
🛏   HOTEL/MOTEL
✆   PHONE
👫   RESTROOM

FR
44

BEULAH

WILDELL

FR
44

NORTH

SCALE IN MILES

0   1/2   1

(MAP 2B
CONTINUES
FROM HERE)

Rail Trails along the Greenbrier River   37

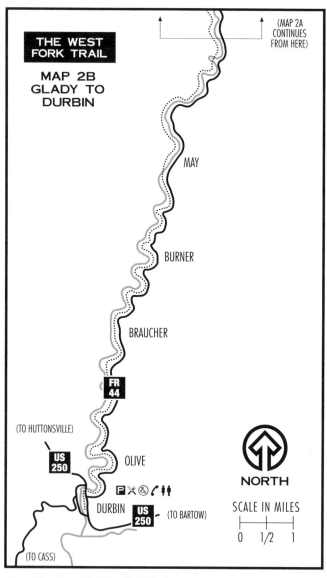

THE WEST
FORK TRAIL

MAP 2B
GLADY TO
DURBIN

(MAP 2A
CONTINUES
FROM HERE)

MAY

BURNER

BRAUCHER

FR 44

(TO HUTTONSVILLE)

US 250

OLIVE

DURBIN   US 250   (TO BARTOW)

(TO CASS)

NORTH

SCALE IN MILES

0   1/2   1

that are hard packed. It appears that the trout-stocking truck has compacted the cinders and gravel along this stretch, improving the surface for bikers.

If you begin to ride the West Fork Trail and discover the slow going is eating up your time, I suggest crossing over to FR 44. On FR 44 you'll find that the hard-packed clay and gravel make for excellent riding and will allow you to increase your pace. In fact, the best way to ride the West Fork trail is in a series of loops based on access points along FR 44. Ride down the trail and back up the road. By camping at Wildell, you should be able to ride the trail into Glady and return along FR 44 in a day. A second day would be enough for the loop from Wildell to May. A third day and you could finish the trail.

PART THREE
The Greenbrier River Trail
✳ ✳ ✳
CHAPTER EIGHT
An Overview of the Trail

In July 1899, construction began on what was to become the Greenbrier Division of the C & O Railroad. The first official train to travel to Marlinton on the new line arrived on October 26, 1900. By January 22, 1901, the line was open from Whitcomb to Cass. Later it extended up the East Fork of the Greenbrier River to Winterburn. For the next 77 years, this railroad served the local lumber industry and carried freight and passengers along the Greenbrier River Valley in eastern West Virginia. On December 29, 1978, the last two depots ceased operation and closed their doors.

While discussions were proceeding on the abandonment of the line, other hearings were taking place to give the right-of-way a new life. In the end, the CSX System donated the right-of-way, land, and improvements (with some important exceptions, such as the southern three miles of right-of-way) to West Virginia. In turn, the state agreed to place the right-of-way between Cass and Whitcomb in a "rail bank" so that rail service could be reestablished should it ever become necessary. This same land would be leased to the Department of Natural Resources for recreational use as the Greenbrier River Trail.

The Greenbrier River Trail is 77 miles long and winds from Cass, in Pocahontas County, to North Caldwell, in Greenbrier County. The trail, like most roads and railroads in West Virginia, is seldom straight. The trail's gradient drops from 2,446 feet above sea level at Cass to 1,693 feet at North Caldwell. This gentle drop of 752 feet in 77 miles makes hiking and riding the trail easy. The steepest gradient along the trail (just downriver from Cass) is less than one percent.

The Greenbrier River Trail is one of the better hiking, biking, skiing, and horseback riding trails in West Virginia. The trail is also used by fishermen, swimmers, and canoeists for access to the river. While it can be used for hiking all year long, biking or horseback riding in the winter months can be difficult. Cross country skiing is viable in winter, but requires a minimum of six inches of snow to prevent damage to skis from the protruding railroad ballast, rock and gravel. In addition to the trail itself, visitors are allowed to use the land approximately 50 feet from the center of the trail on either side of the trail. Beyond this the land may be public or private property. If unsure about the status of the property, stay within this approximate 100 foot wide area.

While the entire trail can be biked (or ridden on horseback) in two or three days — or walked in five or six — most people prefer to travel at a more leisurely pace. Therefore, this guide describes the trail in sections of varying lengths, determined by the ease of trail access.

Many of the original mileposts can be seen along the trail. These milepost markers are square concrete posts which come to a point at the top. They resemble small Washington Monuments. The mile number is usually painted on them, but sometimes it is not legible. Several mileposts have been damaged or removed. A few missing mileposts have been replaced with replicas of the originals. Some sources state that the locations of the replacement posts are not 100% accurate. However, these new markers are sufficiently accurate for general use.

Another type of marker is also found on the

Greenbrier River Trail. This second type of markers are similar to the mileposts, but are thinner. These thinner markers have the letter "W" carved and painted on one side. These markers reminded the engineers to sound a signal — consisting of two long, one short, and a final long blast — on their whistles. This signal was to be sounded at all crossings, bridges, tunnels or other places people, vehicles, or animals might cross or obstruct the track. Like the milepost markers, several of these markers have been defaced or are missing. No effort has been made to erect replicas of the whistle markers.

The northern mile or so of the trail still has ties and rails down. This stretch is hard to hike and nearly impossible to bike. The remaining sections of the trail consist of hard-packed dirt, railroad ballast, or limestone chips. Much of this limestone came from the Renick Rock Quarry, near milepost 26.

While hikers have little trouble with the varying surface conditions, bikers will need to vary their speed and riding techniques for the changing trail surfaces. In the late summer of 1995, a two mile stretch of the trail south of the Marlinton depot was blacktopped to make it accessible to those confined to wheel chairs. Floods in 1996 and 1997 eroded the trail surface in the area north of Marlinton, especially between Deer Creek and Sitlington. The majority of the trail in this area is impassable to bicycles. From Sitlington to Marlinton most of the trail can be ridden. South of Marlinton the trail is still in good shape for hikers or bikers except for minor damage. Call one of the State Parks (*see addresses and phone numbers in Appendix I*) to see if repair work has been started before planning to travel over this section of the trail.

Two tunnels exist along the Greenbrier River Trail. Sharps Tunnel is 9 miles north of Marlinton. This tunnel is the longer (511 feet) and straighter of the two. The floor of Sharps Tunnel has been dry and smooth every time I have gone through it. Work began on building Sharps Tunnel in September of 1899, and was completed by November of 1900. This tunnel is easy to ride through, but I usually walk it. On one hike, four of us stayed dry inside the tunnel while lightning flashed and rain cascaded from the sky.

The Droop Mountain Tunnel is just south of the Greenbrier/Pocahontas County line. This tunnel was completed by May of 1900 and has a ten degree curve in its 402 foot length. The floor inside this tunnel is usually covered with standing water and rocks fallen from the ceiling and walls. In September 1992, this tunnel was graded out. If riding the trail, I always walk my bike through Droop Mountain Tunnel. A flashlight is useful when traversing either tunnel.

Numerous bridges carry the trail across many streams, creeks, and the Greenbrier River itself. Three bridges deserve special mention. The bridge crossing the river at Sharps Tunnel was built for its site in 1900 by the Pencoyd Iron Works in Pennsylvania. The four spans total about 230 feet and are of deck plate girder design. The bridge over Knapps Creek (#557) was built by the Passaic Rolling Mill Company in 1889. This bridge originally spanned the Jackson River in Virginia. Each span of the bridge itself is 132 feet long. The southern-most of these three bridges (#479) on the trail crosses the river at Watoga. This bridge was built for the Maysville and Big Sandy Railroad in 1886 by the Phoenix Bridge Company, and later moved to its present location. Originally, both spans were 149' 11," but one was shortened to 128' 6" when the bridge was relocated. The Watoga bridge was damaged in May 1925 and the southern (downriver) span had to be replaced. The new

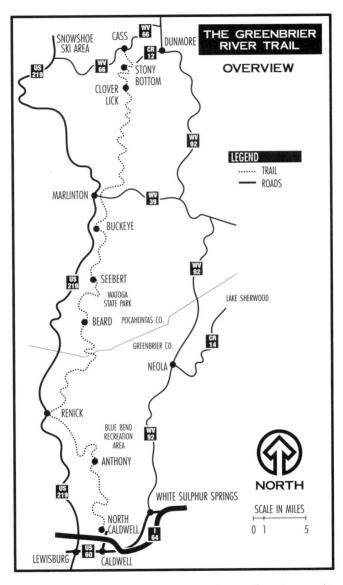

THE GREENBRIER
RIVER TRAIL

OVERVIEW

SNOWSHOE
SKI AREA

CASS

WV
66

DUNMORE

US
219

WV
66

CR
12

STONY
BOTTOM

CLOVER
LICK

WV
92

MARLINTON

WV
39

BUCKEYE

LEGEND
.... TRAIL
——— ROADS

US
219

SEEBERT

WV
92

WATOGA
STATE PARK

LAKE SHERWOOD

BEARD

POCAHONTAS CO.

GREENBRIER CO.

CR
14

NEOLA

RENICK

BLUE BEND
RECREATION
AREA

WV
92

ANTHONY

NORTH

US
219

WHITE SULPHUR SPRINGS

NORTH
CALDWELL

I
64

SCALE IN MILES

0 1   5

US
60

LEWISBURG

CALDWELL

Rail Trails along the Greenbrier River   45

span was built by the American Bridge Company and is 151' 3" long. The other span of this bridge was replaced in 1929 when the other two "used" bridges were replaced.

Although the Greenbrier River Trail is a state park, the trail has not been developed beyond simple maintenance of the trail surface and the establishment of a few primitive camping sites. Most sites consist of a weather-beaten picnic table and a stone fire ring. Since the trail is sandwiched between the river and a hillside or cliff along most of its route, it is difficult to get away from the river to answer a call of nature. Simple pit toilets at each camp site would be welcome additions to the trail. The current improvements along the trail generally consist of occasional stone steps from the trail to the river, and gates across the trail.

The main stem of the Greenbrier River is suitable for open canoes along the full length of the trail. A beautiful spot to put in is at Sitlington Creek, just upstream of the bridge on the side opposite the trail. The run from Sitlington to Marlinton is suitable for novice canoeists if they don't mind getting wet — at times you may have to wade beside the canoe. When planning a canoe trip, be sure you don't bite off more than you can chew. At low water it takes a lot longer to travel downriver. Don't try to squeeze a three day paddle into two. After dark, river running is dangerous and no fun.

While on the trail you should carry water and a snack. Only a few stores lie close to the trail, but those establishments do sell bottled water and soft drinks. Most stores near the trail also have soft drink machines located outside which are available when the store is closed. Don't forget change for phones and soft drink machines.

Located near the northern end of the trail, Cass State

Park has a restaurant and a snack bar in its "old company store." A convenience store is located across the river from the State Park. A service station near Moore's Lodge in Stony Bottom has a soft drink machine. The next stores and restaurants downriver are found in Marlinton, the only major town along the trail. One important store is Appalachian Sports, located just off the trail at 106 Eighth Street in Marlinton. They can satisfy basic equipment needs while you're on the trail.

The next store is McNeill's Country Mart along US 219 at Buckeye, just south of Marlinton. Seven miles further south is Jack Horner's Convenience Store, which replaced the Seebert General Store. Jack Horner (yes, that really is his name) has many items for hikers and campers, and plans to have more. The employees at these two stores have always gone out of their way to make visitors welcome. An employee at McNeill's graciously loaned me a pair of warm, dry socks when I showed up with cold, wet socks and feet.

Two stores within easy reach from the trail are R & V Grocery and Exxon and Field's Gas and Grocery. These two are 20 miles further south at Renick. The last store along the trail is Terrapin Station General Store at Anthony. This recent addition had its grand opening July 4, 1997. So far, the store is mainly selling bait, munchies and soft drinks. The owner plans to expand its services and include bike, boat and canoe rental in the near future.

CHAPTER NINE
Cass to Clover Lick

MILEPOST

95.55	Durbin
80.68	Cass
80.0	Cold Run
79.55	Deer Creek Station
79.0	Deer Creek on east side of river
	Rails and ties remain in place from here to Durbin.
78.46	Raywood
77.8	Moses Run
76.79	Sitlington (Forrest)
	Sitlington Creek on east side of river
74.5	Woods Run
74.37	Stony Bottom
73.8	Elk Lick Run
73.0	Clover Lick Creek/Glade Run
71.17	Clover Lick

In the early 1900's, a railroad was built which ran from the Greenbrier River at present day Cass, up Leatherbark Run, to the top of Cheat Mountain. Called the Greenbrier & Elk Railroad, it later became the Greenbrier, Elk & Valley Railroad, and then the Greenbrier, Cheat & Elk Railroad. In 1961, the West Virginia Legislature appropriated funds for the purchase of 11 miles of track and three engines for the Cass, Greenbrier, Cheat & Bald Knob Scenic Railroad. In late 1962, the name was shortened to Cass Scenic Railroad.

The 4 miles of track from Cass to Whittaker Station (Gum Fields) were opened for passenger traffic on June 15, 1963. Twenty-three thousand people visited Cass State Park during its first year. The next 8 miles of track were open for traffic on May 25, 1968, and allowed travel from Whittaker Station to the top of Bald Knob, the second highest point in West Virginia. Passengers on this 4 hour round trip travel past spectacular scenery, through deciduous woodlands up to Red Spruce forests reminiscent of Canada.

Cass State Park consists of 1,089 acres, most of it a 50 foot strip along the railroad right-of-way up Cheat Mountain. Thirteen cabins are available for rent at the park. The Shay Inn, The Cass Inn, and other nearby establishments also offer additional accommodations. However, because of the large number of people who visit the park, reservations are essential if you want to guarantee a stay in Cass itself.

Cass State Park has a single focus: logging trains. It is not set up for campers or hikers. Overnight parking is not allowed in the large parking lot, and there are no areas set up for long term parking. The closest camping facilities are at Whittaker Campground located off CR 1 (Back Mountain Road) on the way to Stony Bottom. The park has a restaurant, post office, public phones, drinking water, and toilets. There is also a country store, which mainly sells products related to trains.

The Cass end of the Greenbrier River Trail is now marked with a large sign similar to those at other access points. A small gravel parking area near the trail is probably for trail use. I suggest inquiring in the General Store before you leave your vehicle parked overnight. You can get a copy of the park service map and trail guide at the depot or in the country store.

Outdoor enthusiasts may enjoy the hiking, biking and canoeing around Cass. Peters Mountain Trail (TR 359) is a loop that leaves WV 66 (formerly CR 7) just east of Cass. It winds its way across Deer Creek and up to the ridge on top of Peters Mountain. After running

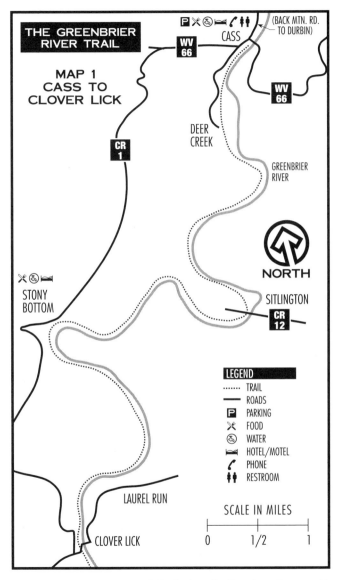

THE GREENBRIER
RIVER TRAIL

MAP 1
CASS TO
CLOVER LICK

WV 66

CR 1

CR 12

CASS

(BACK MTN. RD.
TO DURBIN)

WV 66

DEER
CREEK

GREENBRIER
RIVER

NORTH

SITLINGTON

STONY
BOTTOM

LEGEND
········· TRAIL
———— ROADS
P PARKING
✕ FOOD
Ⓐ WATER
⊨ HOTEL/MOTEL
☎ PHONE
†† RESTROOM

LAUREL RUN

CLOVER LICK

SCALE IN MILES

0   1/2   1

along the ridge it drops to WV 92 about .5 mile from the intersection with WV 66. Bar Ford Trail (TR 370) takes a turn at 3 miles from the west end of Peters Mountain Trail, descends Clay Hollow, and re-crosses Deer Creek to WV 66 at .5 mile from the beginning of Peters Mountain Trail.

The Allegheny Trail (TR 701) joins the Greenbrier River Trail at Cass and accompanies it to Sitlington. There it turns east and travels along Sitlington Road (CR 12) for about 1 mile. Several trails connect the Greenbrier River Trail with the Allegheny Trail. The Allegheny Trail is to be used for hiking only. It was not designed or constructed for mountain bikes or horses, and they are not recommended or welcome on it.

If you are traveling upriver, the Greenbrier River Trail seems to disappear just south of Deer Creek. First the ties reappear, then the rails. Shortly afterwards the edges of the right of way have washed out. Hikers have little problem with this stretch of trail, but it's dangerous for mountain bikes. Bikers should skip this stretch by bypassing it on the country roads. Riders going south will find this easy to do by going right out asphalt WV 66 for .5 mile. Next go left onto Deer Creek Road (CR 1/13). Deer Creek is a well-packed gravel road that is fairly level and easy to ride. It ends at the old Deer Creek stop, .5 mile from the WV 66 intersection. This is the best route for beginners or those who cannot face a steep hill.

Those who don't mind climbing steep hills can continue out WV 66 another mile to the top of the mountain. Here WV 66 bears right and CR 1 turns left. Follow CR 1, also known as Back Mountain Road, downhill for the next 3 to 4 miles until it reaches the river and trail at Stony Bottom. Back Mountain Road is narrow, so beware of cars and trucks. They seldom slow for bikers.

A small motel, Moore's Lodge, is located at Stony Bottom. You'll also find a soft drink machine at a service station a short distance uphill past the trail on CR 1. This is your last chance to buy a cold drink until you get to Marlinton. As at Cass, there is no designated parking area at Stony Bottom.

Floods have washed away the trail surface from just below Deer Creek south to Sitlington, leaving the trail nearly impossible to ride. Even an expert could have problems in some areas with the sudden drop-offs and huge boulders. Until this area is repaired I suggest it be avoided. South of Sitlington the flood damage is more localized, and long stretches can be ridden. But you should expect to walk your bike over some areas. Call one of the State Parks (*see addresses and phone numbers in Appendix I*) to see if repair work has been started before planning to bike over this section of the trail.

The present bridge at Sitlington replaced the bridge which washed out in the 1985 flood. For a good campsite, cross the bridge and go a very short distance up graveled Sitlington Road (CR 12). A dirt road branches off here and winds downhill to Sitlington Creek. Just across this creek is a popular spot for launching canoes. I don't know who owns this piece of land, but it is commonly used for camping and river access.

Just below the Sitlington Bridge are several private camps which soon give way to a finger of Seneca State Forest. Most of Seneca State Forest's 11,684 acres lie across the river from the trail. The State Forest ends before you get to Stony Bottom. It has seven rustic cabins and ten tent/trailer sites a few miles from the trail. Camp Seneca was originally a Civilian Conservation Corps facility, located at the eastern end of the present State Forest.

Naturalists will enjoy taking their time along this section of the trail because of its abundant wildlife. I have seen numerous ground hogs, deer, snakes, squirrels, chipmunks, and other animals in this area. On one trip, a six foot black snake sped off the trail as we approached. Keep your eyes open.

CHAPTER TEN
Clover Lick to Marlinton

MILEPOST

71.17	Clover Lick
71.1	Bridge piers from Raine Lumber Company (1913-1929)
70.11	Camper
69.6	Campsite east side of trail
67.4	Big Run (Lombardy)
65.28	West Portal of Sharps Tunnel (511 feet long)
64.55	Harter
63.7	Campsite east side of trail
62.11	Clawson
61.02	Thorny Creek
60.25	August
59.46	Halfway Run bridge
59.4	Halfway Run
59.36	Knapp (Sixty)
57.44	Greenbrier River Lumber Co. Siding
56.96	Marlinton and Camden Railroad Junction
56.5	Only remaining railroad water tower along the trail
56.13	Marlinton Depot

Clover Lick to Marlinton is an easy section of the trail to hike, bike, ride, or ski. During October 1995, the old Clover Lick Depot building was moved to the north side of the road crossing. For years it had lain in disrepair in a nearby field. It is currently being refurbished as an information center, complete with water source, for trail users. Flooding during early 1996 has delayed its opening.

At milepost 69.6 you'll find the first improved campsite along the trail. This site has a picnic table,

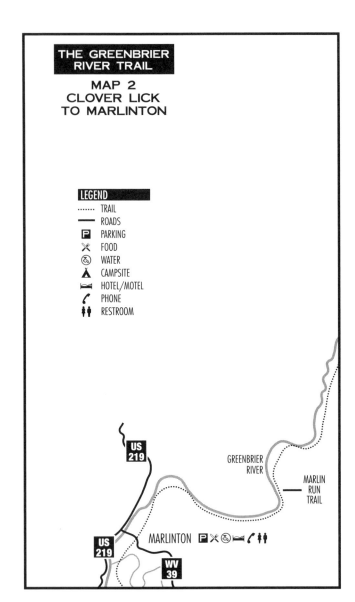

THE GREENBRIER
RIVER TRAIL

MAP 2
CLOVER LICK
TO MARLINTON

LEGEND
.... TRAIL
——— ROADS
🅿 PARKING
✕ FOOD
♿ WATER
⛺ CAMPSITE
🛏 HOTEL/MOTEL
☎ PHONE
🚻 RESTROOM

US 219

GREENBRIER
RIVER

MARLIN
RUN
TRAIL

US 219

MARLINTON 🅿✕♿🛏☎🚻

WV 39

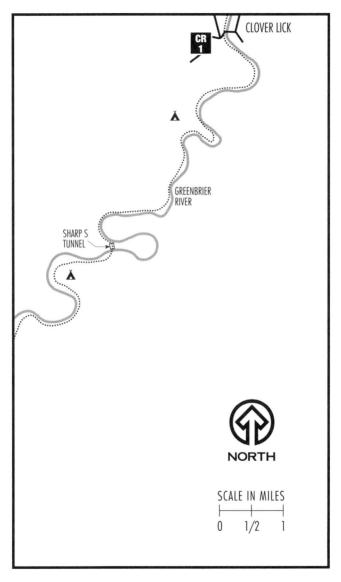

CLOVER LICK

CR 1

GREENBRIER RIVER

SHARP S TUNNEL

NORTH

SCALE IN MILES

0   1/2   1

loose fire ring of native river stone, and good river access. There is no trash can or toilet facility here. This campsite is surrounded by a heavy growth of ferns. Near milepost 69.6 we watched the cottony white flash of a deer's tail as it bounded down the trail in front of us. When it found a spot to its liking, it turned and plunged over the hill to the river. Within seconds it was gone from sight. Further south, near Big Run, we saw an adult beaver slap the water and disappear in a small pond. The last two of our party stopped for a break. The rest of us rode on and saw a beaver kit follow when it thought the coast was clear.

At one time there was a dangerous flood-damaged section of trail just upriver from Sharps Tunnel. This area had been repaired, but subsequent floods have caused more damage. Culverts placed under the trail were washed out in early 1996, along with the top eighteen inches or so of new gravel. The culverts can be seen scattered downriver below this area. While this stretch can be ridden and is not dangerous, it is not up to rail road grade standards.

The first major bridge along the trail is just downriver from Sharps Tunnel. This bridge across the Greenbrier was built for the site in 1900 by the Pencoyd Iron Works in Pennsylvania. Its four spans total about 230 feet, and the bridge is of deck plate girder design. The south end of the bridge has a step-like retaining wall flanking its right side. This is a good place to climb down to the river and wet your feet for a few minutes. A cleared spot here could serve as a campsite. However, this spot is popular for fishing. If you camp here, you might expect to be woken by night fishermen.

The second improved campsite along the trail, at milepost 63.7, has a picnic table and a loose fire ring made of local stone. There is no river access, toilet facility, or trash can.

An unimproved road runs along the river between August and Knapp, where the road turns up Halfway Run to the top of Marlin Mountain. This section of road that parallels the trail has been rutted and muddy each time I've seen it. The mud can be bypassed by staying on the Greenbrier River Trail until just south of Halfway Run.

At Halfway Run, a Forest Service sign (positioned for those coming off the hillside) indicates it is 6 miles north to Sharps Tunnel, and 3 miles south to Marlinton. Marlinton Mountain Loop crosses Marlin Mountain to the headwaters of Marlin Run and Marlin Run Trail (TR 418), which it follows into Marlinton. It is possible to get turned around on the many jeep trails in the area. Be aware of your surroundings and use a topo map. Gil and Mary Willis describe the Marlin Mountain Loop in their booklet, *Mountain Bike Rides in Pocahontas County, West Virginia*.

As you ride into Marlinton, you'll see a water tower on your left. This is the only remaining railroad water tower along the trail. This is the second water tower to serve the railroad in Marlinton. The first was located between Eighth and Ninth Street south of the depot. Like its predecessor, the "new" tank is twenty-four feet in diameter and sixteen feet high. It holds 50,000 gallons of water. Today the tank has a jungle of weeds growing around it, so don't plan to picnic in its shade.

The depot in Marlinton was deeded to the Marlinton Railroad Depot, Incorporated. It was entered on the National Register of Historic Places on August 29, 1979. Today, the Pocahontas County Tourism Commission and Visitors Center occupies a portion of the depot.

Here you can get information on Pocahontas County, use rest rooms and get water.

Marlinton is big enough to offer many convenient facilities while you are on the trail. You'll find public phones, a post office, the Pocahontas Memorial Hospital, several motels, stores, and a wide range of restaurants. The major food stores are Fas-Chek, Foodland, and Little General Store. Several restaurants are conveniently located near the trail: French's Diner, Godfather's Pizza, and The River Place Restaurant. A number of other eating establishments are located along US 219 across the river from the trail.

Appalachian Sports is located just off the trail at 106 Eighth Street. They carry the basic supplies for camping, hunting, fishing and cycling. The only other place on the trail to get bike parts is Jack Horner's in Seebert. The owner at Appalachian Sports will assist customers with minor repairs and adjustments. They also rent mountain bikes and canoes.

Chapter Eleven
Marlinton to Buckeye

MILEPOST

56.13   Marlinton Depot
55.71   Knapps Creek Bridge West Pier
55.7   Mouth of Knapps Creek
55.2   Stillwell Park Campsite
55.06   Stillwell
55.0   Stillhouse Run
54.97   Burrus Lumber Company Siding (Now the site
        of the W. M. Cramer Lumber Company)
54.1   Sunday Lick Run
53.93   Munday Lick Station
53.9   Monday Lick Run
52.5   Swago Creek on west side of river
52.18   Buckeye

The shortest section of the trail, the 4 mile stretch from Marlinton to Buckeye is a good hike for an afternoon. The first 2 miles of this stretch were black-topped during the late summer of 1995 to increase its wheelchair accessibility. While this section starts among the residences of Marlinton, it quickly leaves the houses behind and abounds in great scenery. The sheer number and variety of spring and summer wildflowers along this stretch are amazing.

Leaving Marlinton, you'll cross the bridge over Knapps Creek (#557). The bridge was built by the Passaic Rolling Mill Company in 1889, and originally spanned the Jackson River in Virginia. The bridge's spans are each 132 feet long. The bridge, which had to be replaced in 1929, connects the town of Marlinton to its city park at Stillwell.

Hikers and other trail users are allowed to camp in

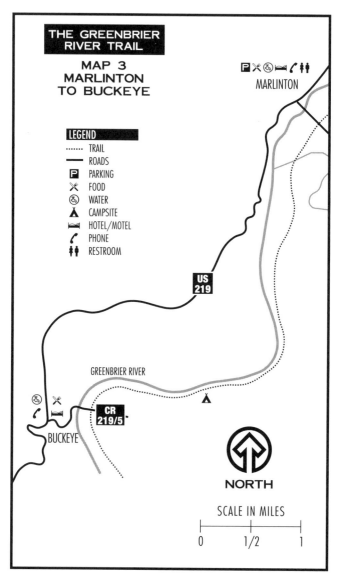

THE GREENBRIER
RIVER TRAIL

MAP 3
MARLINTON
TO BUCKEYE

MARLINTON

LEGEND
- ········· TRAIL
- —— ROADS
- 🅿 PARKING
- ✗ FOOD
- ♲ WATER
- 🛆 CAMPSITE
- 🛏 HOTEL/MOTEL
- ✆ PHONE
- 👫 RESTROOM

US
219

GREENBRIER RIVER

CR
219/5

BUCKEYE

NORTH

SCALE IN MILES

0   1/2   1

Stillwell Park for a small fee per tent. Recreational vehicles are not allowed. There is a one week limit on camping here. I suspect trail users would also be allowed to park their vehicles here for similar periods of time while they are using the trail. This park has public toilets, water, picnic tables, ball fields, and recreational equipment.

The Marlinton-Buckeye section of the trail has two connections to Buckley Mountain Trail (TR 425), which is part of the Allegheny Trail (TR 701). Buckley Mountain Trail runs along the crest of Buckley Mountain about 3 miles east of the river. The first connection is the light duty road up the left side of Stillhouse Run (FR 303). Stillhouse Run dead ends at Buckley Mountain Trail along the ridge on top of Buckley Mountain. The second connection is another light duty road (FR 1002) which continues south along the Greenbrier River Trail, past Sunday Lick Run to Monday Lick Run, where it turns up the mountain. This road becomes unimproved at a cemetery on the ridge. A short distance further it connects to Buckley Mountain Trail. A gate blocks this road, at least part of the time.

Just before you reach Buckeye, there is a former section house. A section house was a company-owned home where the section foreman resided. Each section foreman oversaw maintenance along a section of railroad, usually about ten miles in length. A short distance past the section house, a locking post has been erected to prevent cars from driving north along the trail.

There are several commercial facilities along US 219 at Buckeye. One I mentioned earlier, McNeill's Country Mart & Ashland Station. Here you're likely to find employees who'd give you the shirt off their back, if not the socks off their feet. Such kindness should be rewarded in heaven, if not before.

At a roadside park in Buckeye you'll find picnic tables, trash cans and public toilets. Buckeye also has a public phone, post office, and Graham's Motel. To reach these facilities, turn right off the trail at Buckeye and cross the narrow bridge. Continue along CR 219/5 until you have a choice of turning left or right. This is about .5 mile from the trail. Turn left for another .1 mile and you will be on US 219. You should be able to see just about all of the facilities in Buckeye from the intersection of US 219 and CR 219/5.

The intersection of US 219 and CR 219/5 is in a dangerous curve. Use caution when crossing here. There are very few parking spots close to the trail at Buckeye. The area has the reputation for being a local hangout for kids, and you'll usually find empty beer cans or bottles scattered around. To be cautious, I don't leave my vehicle here.

CHAPTER TWELVE
Buckeye to Seebert

MILEPOST

52.18	Buckeye
50.1	Improvement Lick Run Trestle
49.3	Mouth of Beaver Creek campsite west of trail
49.3	Beaver Creek
49.23	Violet (Dan)
48.10	Watoga foundations of the lumber camp and bank safe can be seen east of the trail.
47.9	Trail crosses to west bank on Watoga Bridge (287 feet).
47.8	Webster Run enters the river on the eastern side.
47.1	Stevens Hole Run
46.6	Stamping Creek
46.32	Warns
45.77	Seebert

The Buckeye to Seebert section of the trail is surfaced with hard-packed gravel. It winds past small summer camps and remote farm land. There are no major developments along the way. The first .2 mile of this section is used as a right-of-way to the large farmhouse at milepost 52. Cyclists frequently combine this section with the Marlinton to Buckeye section for a comfortable day's round trip.

North of milepost 51 is a large grassy clearing beside a small stream. This clearing is not a designated camp-site, but a re-seeded quarry where rock was obtained to rebuild flood damaged portions of the trail.

The bridge over Improvement Lick Creek at milepost 50.1 has been replaced since 1992. The new bridge has large gaps between the cross ties, making it hard to ride.

To protect your wheels, I suggest walking your bike across it. Just below the creek to your left, in the yard of the Pomeroy's camp, is a sign that indicates the high water mark from the 1985 flood.

The campsite north of the mouth of Beaver Creek (milepost 50.1) is my favorite of all the "improved" campsites, although the only improvements are a picnic table and a loose fire ring of river stone. The rock bass in the backwater beside the trail are fun to catch. They'll hit on any small lure, as long as it's a black jig.

Usually, I spend the night here and have what Louis L'Amour would call a "hat full of fire" to keep me company. There is (unfortunately) usually enough trash here to start a fire, and enough squaw wood to keep it going for a few hours. Immediately below the campsite is the large iron bridge over Beaver Creek.

If you keep a close eye out, from the trail you can still see the remains of the town of Watoga. One interesting landmark to look for is the safe used by the lumber company, and located in what used to be the company store. The easiest way to find signs of the town is to locate milepost 48, and then go north about .1 mile until you reach the first gate on your right. Just past it is the rear of the safe. From the rear it appears to be a square block structure about fifteen feet high. The rusty door is about eight feet off the ground and still swings on its hinges. Several paths wander through the old overgrown town site, which is now private property. Little can be seen beyond the foundation stones and the bank safe. The old fruit trees in the area indicate the extent of the town.

Bridge #479 carries the trail to the west side of the river just below Watoga. It is the southernmost major bridge along the trail. This bridge was built for the Maysville and Big Sandy Railroad in 1886 by the

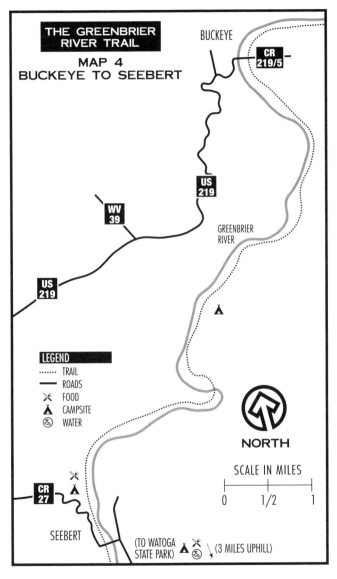

THE GREENBRIER
RIVER TRAIL

MAP 4
BUCKEYE TO SEEBERT

BUCKEYE

CR
219/5

US
219

WV
39

US
219

GREENBRIER
RIVER

LEGEND

······· TRAIL
——— ROADS
✕ FOOD
▲ CAMPSITE
♿ WATER

NORTH

SCALE IN MILES

0   1/2   1

CR
27

SEEBERT

(TO WATOGA
STATE PARK) ▲ ✕ ♿ ↓ (3 MILES UPHILL)

Phoenix Bridge Company. Later it was moved to its present location. Originally, both spans were 149' 11" but one was shortened to 128' 6" when the bridge was relocated. This bridge was damaged in May 1925 and the downriver span was replaced. The new span was built by the American Bridge Company and is 151' 3" long. The other span was replaced in 1929.

After crossing the bridge, you'll find a short path to the left that leads down to a sloping rock ledge with nice, level areas. This ledge is an excellent place for a lunch, swimming, fishing, or a nap. The water here is clear enough to watch the small bass and other fish dart after bread crumbs.

Jack Horner's Corner Convenience Store in Seebert is only a few yards to the right of the trail at about mile-post 46. The heavy brush that once hid it has been cut. The store is between the trail and the two-lane asphalt road (CR 27) through town. Jack Horner — Senior and Junior — have great plans for this store that will benefit trail users. They have begun selling bottled water, bike repair items, tools, fishing equipment, Coleman fuel, and microwave dinners. Yes, they have a microwave oven for customers to use. They rent bicycles, as well as inner tubes for swimming. They have plans to begin renting basic camping items such as sleeping bags, tents, and Coleman stoves. Trail users will be allowed to camp in the narrow space between the store and the trail. Hikers and bikers will be able to make arrangements to spend Saturday night here and not carry all their supplies on a weekend trip. They even have indoor toilets for their customers. What else could a camper want?

Jack Horner, Senior has operated the stables at nearby Watoga State Park for years. He knows the history of the area extremely well. Even if you aren't going to rent a bike or other equipment, a chat with

Jack is worth the stop. The signs for Seebert are located at mileposts 47 and 45.7. Watoga State Park, near Seebert, is close to the halfway point along the trail. There are many trails and fire roads through the park that provide opportunities for circuit hikes, cross country skiing, and rides. For more information, check with Jack Horner, or see the next chapter.

CHAPTER THIRTEEN
Seebert to Beard

MILEPOST

45.77	Seebert
44.2	Across river is Riverside Campground
42.96	Kennison
41.70	Burnsides
40.89	Mill Run Station. Campsite on old siding
39.4	Denmar State Correctional Facility. Foundations and bridge piers from Maryland Lumber Company (1910-1918).
39.33	Denmar (Den Mar)
38.48	Beard (Beards)

The Seebert to Beard section is relatively isolated. Once you are south of Seebert, the trail is sandwiched between the hillside and the river until you reach Denmar. Located near Seebert is Watoga State Park. The park's 10,100 acres lie to the east of the river while the trail follows the west bank. The park extends from milepost 45.2 to 39.2. Watoga has eight deluxe cabins, twenty-five standard cabins, and 88 campsites for rent.

Like most state parks, Watoga has a number of hiking trails. Most of these trails intersect, making several circuit hikes possible. North Boundary Road has gates at each end and connects to Monongaseneka Trail, Bear Pen Run Trail, Buck & Doe Trail, and Allegheny Trail, for hikes with a variety of lengths. None of these trails connect directly to the Greenbrier River Trail. There is at least a river in between. Especially notable among the Watoga Trails are the three Arboretum Trails: Dragon Draft, Buckhorn and Honeybee. Many of the trees and plants along the Arboretum Trails are labeled to assist the hiker in identifying them.

The park office has a map of all the hiking trails in Watoga, as well as one solely for the three Arboretum Trails. Watoga also has a restaurant and store at the park office located some three miles up hill from the trail. Water and showers at the Riverside Campground, two miles south of the bridge at Seebert, are reserved for use by campers staying there.

Camp Watoga, a Civilian Conservation Corps camp, was located along Beaver Creek in what is now the maintenance area of Watoga State Park. It operated in 1933 and 1934 as a state forest camp. When Watoga State Forest became Watoga State Park, it became a state park camp and operated until 1942. A second CCC facility, Camp Seebert, was located at the mouth of Island Lick Run in Watoga State Park, about where the campgrounds are located today. A third CCC camp, Camp Will Rogers, was located on Laurel Run at the south entrance to Watoga State Park. This is close to the border between Watoga and Calvin Price State Forest.

Calvin Price State Forest, named for the former editor of the Pocahontas Times, is across the river between mileposts 39.2 and 38.0. Its 9,482 acres border Watoga State Park on the south. Only 93 of these acres have been developed for primitive camping and picnicking. The lack of development, and the forest's remoteness, are Calvin Price's greatest attractions.

To get to or return from Calvin Price Forest, cross the river at a ford near Burnsides. Next follow an unimproved road downriver to a second ford back to the trail at Denmar. Use care when crossing the river, especially during the spring and fall, because the water can be deceptively high and fast.

About a mile below Burnsides, at Mill Run Station, is a campsite on the right side of the trail. The campsite is located on the old rail siding. Most of this level area

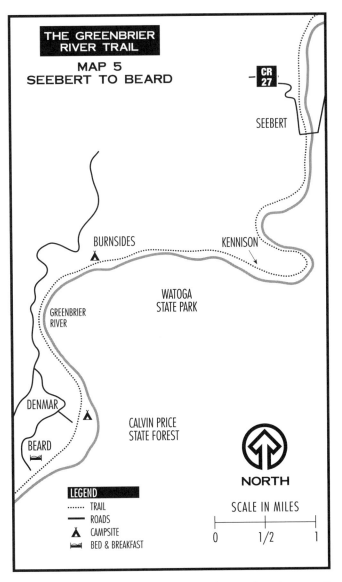

THE GREENBRIER
RIVER TRAIL

MAP 5
SEEBERT TO BEARD

CR
27

SEEBERT

KENNISON

BURNSIDES

WATOGA
STATE PARK

GREENBRIER
RIVER

DENMAR

CALVIN PRICE
STATE FOREST

BEARD

NORTH

LEGEND
········· TRAIL
———— ROADS
▲ CAMPSITE
🛏 BED & BREAKFAST

SCALE IN MILES

0   1/2   1

consists of a thin layer of dirt over gravel. A fire ring and a picnic table constitute the only facilities. It does have excellent river access and a level but hard camping area. The sound of Mill Run cascading down to the river would lull an insomniac to sleep.

The old "Denmar Sanitarium for the Tubercuotic Colored People" became the "Denmar State Hospital for the Chronically Ill" before it closed in 1990. In early 1994, the large white building sprouted barbed wire and became a state correctional facility. Currently the correctional facility can house about 150 inmates. If the other buildings on the grounds were renovated, the facility could house twice that number. There are plans to use part of the hundred acre facility as a "boot camp" type facility for juvenile offenders sometime in the future.

The trail here is bordered by a large cornfield and the sewage treatment plant for the correctional facility. Prison officials discourage parking and camping in the immediate area. Formerly rough and overgrown, the section of trail between Denmar and Beard has been re-graded with limestone chips.

The Current Bed and Breakfast is conveniently located for trail travelers, as it is only .25 mile from the trail. Built in 1905, it originally was the old Beard Farmhouse. Its four guest rooms, three baths, and an outdoor hot tub offer a taste of luxury for trail users. Smoking is not allowed in the house and the meals are semi-vegetarian. The Current makes an excellent overnight stop for those traveling from one end of the trail to the other. Reservations are recommended, and can be made by calling (304) 653-4722.

CHAPTER FOURTEEN
Beard to Renick

MILEPOST

38.48	Beard (Beards)
37.40	Locust (Breakneck, Locust Creek)
36.03	Spice Run Station
35.7	Bridge piers from Spice Run Lumber Co. (1913-1926)
35.4	Spice Run enters on east side of river.
35.4	Boundary between Greenbrier and Pocahontas Counties
33.7	Campsite left side of trail
32.10	Droop Mountain Station
30.91	Droop Mountain Tunnel (402 Feet)
30.62	Rorer
29.64	Horrock
28.5	Campsite left side of trail
28.18	Golden
25.81	Renick Stone Company Tipple
25.5	Old quarry on right. Parking at end of hard road.
24.77	Renick
24.7	CR 11 (Auto Road) Renick Public Fishing Access Area

The Beard to Renick stretch of the Greenbrier River Trail is probably its most remote section. Hence, some trail users will find it their favorite. The station depots along this section have disappeared, as have the lumber companies they served. Most of the former stations are now little more than collections of summer camps.

An unmarked ford to Spice Ridge Trail (TR 621) on the east side of the river is located near the old bridge piers of the former Spice Run Lumber Company. Spice

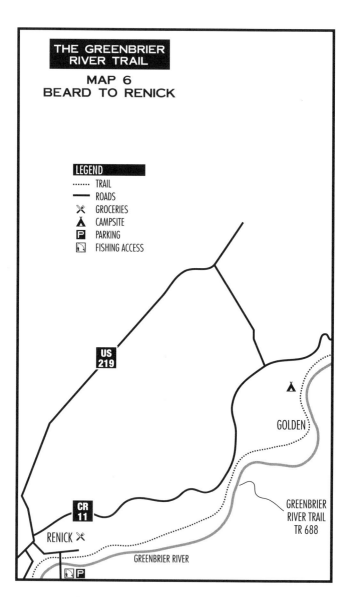

THE GREENBRIER RIVER TRAIL

MAP 6
BEARD TO RENICK

LEGEND
- ········· TRAIL
- —— ROADS
- ✕ GROCERIES
- ⛺ CAMPSITE
- 🅿 PARKING
- 🖼 FISHING ACCESS

US 219

⛺

GOLDEN

CR 11

RENICK ✕

GREENBRIER RIVER TRAIL TR 688

GREENBRIER RIVER

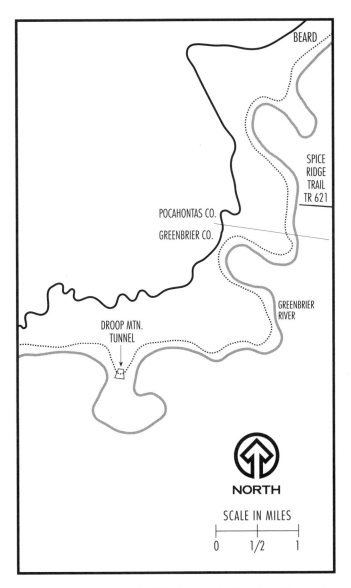

BEARD

SPICE
RIDGE
TRAIL
TR 621

POCAHONTAS CO.

GREENBRIER CO.

GREENBRIER
RIVER

DROOP MTN.
TUNNEL

NORTH

SCALE IN MILES

0   1/2   1

Ridge Trail is a strenuous 12 mile trail that connects with a network of jeep trails, hiking trails, and unimproved roads in Calvin Price State Forest, Watoga State Park, and the Monongahela National Forest.

One publication for canoeists advises against using this area to put in or take out, warning that locals around Spice Run do not welcome canoeists. I have not had a problem using the trail in this area. However, I have never tried driving into the trail here. I have recently heard that the road into Spice Run is a private road, which would account for problems in the area.

At milepost 36 you will come across another trestle with wide spaces between the cross pieces. I suggest you walk over it. At milepost 33.7 you'll find a pleasant campsite that is clearly visible from the trail. It has the standard picnic table, trash can, and fire ring of loose river rock. Its rocky surface makes it undesirable as a sleeping site, but it does have some grazing for horses and easy river access. About .1 mile below this campsite is a private camp. Across the trail from this camp is an "unapproved" spring. Water taken from it should be treated.

Droop Mountain Tunnel is the southernmost of the two tunnels on the Greenbrier River Trail. It lies just south of the Greenbrier/Pocahontas County line at milepost 30.91. The tunnel was completed by May 1900 and has a ten degree curve in its 402 foot length. Until recently, the floor inside Droop Mountain Tunnel has always been covered with standing water and fallen rocks. It has been improved, but it is still damp and rocks fall on a regular basis. A flashlight is recommended when traversing either tunnel. To keep your feet dry in Droop Mountain Tunnel a flashlight is a necessity. It is possible to ride through this tunnel, but I don't. Just below the mouth of Droop Mountain Tunnel is CR 7/2, which serves the summer camps and homes in Rorer and Horrock.

I have heard reports of some flood damage to the trail south of the Droop Mountain Tunnel. My friend George Dasher rode this section recently and said the trail was suitable for riding from Marlinton to the end. At worst, a short part of this section may not be up to railroad grade standards.

The campsite at milepost 28.5 is a grassy bank at a deep water hole. This site has a picnic table, a trash can, and a few fire rings of loose river stone. The grassy bank and easy river access make this an excellent site for horses. This campsite is heavily used by fishermen, but I have never seen anyone else use it. On trips from Marlinton to North Caldwell, I usually camp here overnight. For one of my favorite day trips, I drive from Charleston to Renick, hike to this site for a swim and picnic, and return to Charleston late the same day.

Just south of Golden there is a ford across to Snodgrass Run. You'll also find a series of jeep trails and unimproved roads, as well as another Greenbrier River Trail (TR 688) which runs from near Auto to the river. Big Run Trail (TR 683) connects to TR 688, runs back down Big Run to the river, continues downriver to Boggs Run, and ends with a paved road into Renick. If you find Big Run Trail in guide books, check the information closely. There are at least three trails with that name in the Monongahela National Forest.

All of these trails connect to Laurel Run Trail (TR 679), Civil War Trail (TR 685), Blueline Trail (TR 680), Peach Orchard Trail (TR 616), and other hiking trails in the vicinity of the Blue Bend Recreational Area.

As you ride through Renick, an asphalt road (CR 11 or Auto Road) crosses the trail. To your left is a new bridge over the Greenbrier River. About .5 mile to your right is the intersection with US 219. A quarter mile north of this intersection is Field's Gas and Grocery and the post office. A few hundred yards south is R & V Grocery and Exxon. Public phones, clean rest rooms, and bottled water are available here.

Just past Auto Road, you'll find the "Renick Public Fishing Access Area" at an old service station. Parking for about six vehicles is possible between the trail and the river.

CHAPTER SIXTEEN
Renick to Anthony

MILEPOST

24.77	Renick
23.9	Limestone cave on right side of trail
21.65	Spring Creek
21.53	Spring Creek Station
17.01	Deeter
16.2	Donaldson Lumber Company bridge piers (1903-1913)
16.12	Woodman
15.5	Greenbrier Youth Camp on east side of river
14.12	Anthony

This stretch of the trail is not one of my favorites. The trail is a good distance from the river, and the scenic views are limited because the trees crowd the trail. On the other hand, the variety of habitat along this stretch hosts a broad range of wildflowers and other plants.

Between Renick and Spring Creek the trail runs through a cow pasture. There are no gates, no fences, no signs. Just boom, cattle all over the trail. At times the cattle have run from me. Once I started with over a dozen lumbering down the trail ahead of me. Every time I stopped to let them get off the trail they simply stopped and turned to stare at me. When I started riding, they started running. Every so often one or two of them would take a path to the bottom between the trail and the river. By the time I got to the bridge at Spring Creek I was down to five or six. They wouldn't cross the bridge. As suddenly as they appeared, they disappeared. Once when we rode this section we saw one lone cow lying in the shade along the trail. She didn't get up until we had ridden past her. Even if you

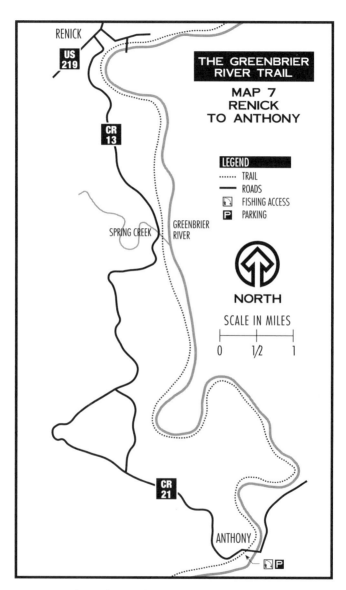

don't see cattle along this section you will see — or smell — reminders of them. This is the least enjoyable section of the trail. Fortunately, an alternative exists. An attractive one.

As you ride through Renick, Auto Road (CR 11) crosses the trail. To your left is the new bridge over the Greenbrier. Ride up the steep hill to your right about .5 mile to US 219. A few 100 yards to your left is R & V Grocery and Exxon. Beside R & V Grocery is Spring Creek Station Road (CR 13). This is a one lane asphalt road gently rising through rolling farm land. Suddenly it plunges downhill to the trail at Spring Creek. At the top of this drop off you can see the river stretching in front of you. The trees splitting the pasture to your left conceal the trail.

At the bottom of this hill you cross a bridge over Spring Creek. A few yards to your left is the old railroad bridge which carries the trail. So far you have traveled about 3 miles from R & V Grocery. Cross the bridge and go up the hill about 100 yards, to the asphalt and gravel road just past the first farmhouse on the left. Take a left on this road for about .25 mile and you are back on the trail.

You have just traded 3 miles of slow gravel trail through a smelly cow pasture for 4 miles of fast road. The road is a little hillier, but a lot more scenic. Another bonus is that it passes a store with public phones, bottled water, and clean rest rooms. Other than the few 100 yards along US 219, traffic is light. In fact, I have seldom seen a moving vehicle on Spring Creek Station Road.

Back on the trail, start watching the high cliffs on the opposite side of the river as you approach milepost 18. A number of large birds fly over this area. I suspect they are hawks of some kind, but I'm not sure. Whatever species they may be, they are beautiful to watch.

Laurel Run Trail (TR 679) is on the east side of the river north of Woodman. This trail ties into Blueline Trail (TR 680), Peach Orchard Trail (TR 616), Civil War Trail (TR 686), and a number of other trails, logging roads, and unimproved roads in the vicinity of Blue Bend Recreational Area. These trails may get periodic maintenance, but I have found the majority were unkempt and unmarked. Peach Orchard is the only one I have managed to hike with any degree of confidence.

The last store along the trail, Terrapin Station General Store at Anthony, lies immediately next to the trail. Its grand opening was July 4, 1997. So far the store is selling mainly bait, munchies and soft drinks. The owner plans to expand into campsites, showers, toilet facilities, bike, boat and canoe rental in the near future. I plan on renting a canoe from him and fishing here on my next trip to the area. Eventually he hopes to have a bed and breakfast and a cabin for rent. Currently, parking is at a premium in the area, as at most of the trail access spots.

Just east of the trail at Anthony, beside the bridge on CR 21/2 and across the road from Terrapin Station, is the "Anthony Public Fishing Access Area." This day use area provides some parking for fishermen as well and trail users. You might get away with parking overnight here for one night. This is also a popular spot for river runners to put in and take out their craft. Jack Dever, one of my college roommates, claims it is an easy two day canoe ride from the bridge at Seebert to Anthony for his Boy Scout troop. Camping is not allowed here, but it is allowed along the South Boundary Trail just across the river.

The South Boundary Trail (TR 615) begins just

across the bridge here and follows the river and Anthony Creek around the end of Gunpowder Ridge. Just above a deep clear water hole, the trail crosses Anthony Creek to the south end of a level bench. South Boundary Trail also crosses Anthony Creek Trail (TR 618) here. Anthony Creek Trail in turn connects with Blue Bend Loop Trail (TR 614) a few miles up Anthony Creek. The South Boundary Trail continues across the mountain to the east until it reaches Big Draft Road near White Sulphur. Across Big Draft Road, Coles Mountain Trail (TR 612) continues for 2 miles.

Years ago, I rode part of the future South Boundary Trail in the back of a station wagon, to the pool of water just below the ford. We called it Crystal Hole. At the time it was well over my head. The last time I was there it was only about five feet deep. It is an ideal place to swim, even if it is icy cold much of the time.

CHAPTER SEVENTEEN
Anthony to North Caldwell

MILEPOST

14.12	Anthony and Anthony Public Fishing and Boat Launch Area
13.4	Anthony Creek enters river on east side.
13.2	Dodson Branch
13.0	Campsite along river
11.08	Keister
9.32	Brink
8.71	Loopemount
7.29	Bowes
5.55	Hopper (or Harper)
4.9	Campsite on east side of trail
3.54	Camp Allegheny (Tottens)
3.3	Southern end of Trail
3.06	Beginning point for 1978 track abandonment
2.8	Howard Creek enters on east side of the river. At one time a ferry existed here.
1.82	North Caldwell Station (Little Sulphur, Hunter)

Most of the Anthony to North Caldwell trail section consists of dense woods which are squeezed between cliffs and river. Just below Dodson Branch, a developer is going to put in condominiums. It appears the developer had gotten as far as laying out the roads. As these lots sell (or get leased) this area should expand tremendously. The trail section ends by paralleling a blacktop county road. It is a good stretch of trail for a day's travel. Along this stretch I have seen three deer, two rabbits, and one groundhog or whistle pig. I saw all these animals in the middle of the morning on the same trip.

The campsite at milepost 13 is located at the base of a cliff with a number of springs gently falling over it.

This campsite has the only fireplace along the trail that is cemented together rather than being made of loose stones. This site also has a nice level spot to pitch a tent beside a deep water hole. All in all, this is a great site.

Keister, Brink, and Loopemount, like many other former stops, are now no more than trail crossings with a few scattered camps. Just south of the crossing at Hopper is the Greenbrier County Sanitary Landfill. It is located only a few hundred yards from the trail. I would not have realized it was in such close proximity to the trail if John Tuckwiller, Chairman of the Greenbrier County Solid Waste Authority, had not shown it to me. As close as it is to the trail, I have never noticed any odor, trash or other debris.

At about milepost 5, a large flat rock edges into the river. It is beside a large water hole, and is a favorite spot of mine for sitting, soaking my feet, and thinking. A few 100 yards downriver is the southernmost campsite along the trail. Its location — just a few miles from the southern end of the trail — makes it ideal for trail users who want to finish early the next day to allow time for driving home. Of course, it's also good for those who start late in the day and want to put a few miles behind them before camping.

You are approaching the end of the trail when you notice Camp Allegheny's parking lot on the river side of the trail. You will see the green and white buildings of Camp Allegheny across the river. A short distance later, an asphalt road appears on the right. Look up the hill to your right and you will be able to see the Old Stone House that gives this road its name. This house was the Totten residence, which gave this station its earlier name. Old Stone House Road (CR 38), which is private, runs beside the trail to its end.

The North Caldwell end of the trail is about 1.3

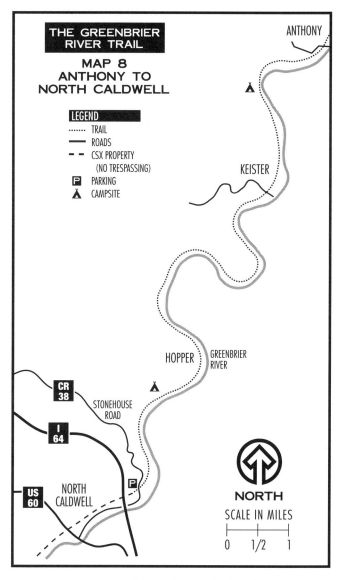

miles north of US 60. Compared to the Cass end, it is sumptuous. It is delineated by square posts, some of which have small yellow signs marking the edge of the trail property. Eight to ten parking spots, two rotting picnic tables, a trash can, and a non-functional water fountain are contained within this small park. A private drive crosses the old railroad right-of-way just past the end of the trail. Private property surrounds the trail end on every side except at the entrance. Trail users should stay within the square posts to prevent trouble with local land owners.

I have spoken to two deputies and a state trooper, on separate occasions, and asked about problems at the trail's end. None had ever heard of problems with any vehicles left there. However, the smart trail user will take the standard precautions anyway.

South of here the old railroad right-of-way is blocked by a mound of tree branches and brush to indicate that walkers are not welcome any further. Although it appears that there are 2 or 3 additional miles of right-of-way to the trail, there are not. Sections of the railroad right of way between the trail's end and Whitcomb have been sold and are not a part of the trail.

Between the Interstate and US 60, a working quarry and a cement plant surround the abandoned track. A number of working roads cross and re-cross this area. One evening I stood on the US 60 bridge over the old right-of-way and watched seven large trucks lumber back and forth preparing for the next day's work. Even if the trail was open in this area, it would be uninviting, if not dangerous, for trail users. You can see the old North Caldwell depot in this area. It was moved from its original site and a basement was added for storage. It appears to be an office building for the quarry or cement plant.

Further south the right of way appears to be plunging into woodland once more. Within 1 mile or so, however, the active railroad line crosses the Greenbrier River and the two right-of-ways join. The trail has gone as far south as it can.

A few miles to the east along US 60 is the North Caldwell or White Sulphur Springs/ Interstate 64 entrance. At this intersection, you'll find several gas stations, food marts, fast food restaurants and other businesses. These facilities are the closest found to the south end of the trail. White Sulphur Springs is also the home of the well-known (and very expensive) resort, The Greenbrier.

Should you go west on US 60 a few miles, you'll come to the town of Lewisburg. In Lewisburg you'll find all kinds of great restaurants, shopping, and The General Lewis Inn. The General Lewis is crammed with antiques and is a charming place to spend the night or stop for supper. My favorite establishment in Lewisburg is What's Cooking, a food and kitchen supply store, located an easy walk west of the General Lewis on Route 60. The owners make fresh cinnamon rolls nearly every day. I always make time to stop in for one or two rolls with a cup of coffee. When leaving the trail, you'll find that the roads CR 38 and US 60, between the trail's end and Interstate 64, are wide, with good shoulders, and a few hills.

PART FOUR
Appendices
* * *
APPENDIX I
Addresses for Maps or Additional Information

These addresses and telephone numbers were verified as of the 1997 telephone books. Businesses have a life cycle just as people do. New ones are being born and old ones move, or die off, often faster than we can keep up with them. Check to see that these establishments still exist, and are at the same location before depending upon them.

This listing is not complete. A number of other businesses in the area could be of interest to hikers or mountain bikers and are not listed here simply because I don't know about them. If you know of a business or organizations you feel should be listed, send it to me in care of Quarrier Press. (Their address is on the front of the book).

Appalachian Sport
Canoe and Mountain Bike Rentals
106 Eighth Street
Marlinton, WV 24954
(304) 799-4050

Cass State Park
Box 107
Cass, WV 24927
(304) 456-4300

The Current Bed and Breakfast
HC 64 Box 135
Hillsboro, WV 24946
(304) 653-4722

DeLorme
West Virginia Atlas & Gazetteer
P. O. Box 298
Yarmouth, Maine 04096
http://www.delorme.com

Elk River Touring Center and Inn
HC 69, Box 7
Slatyfork, WV 26291
(304) 572-3771

Free Spirit Adventures
104 Foster Street
Lewisburg, WV 24901
(304) 645-2093

The Glady Store
Glady, WV 26268
(304) 636-4737

Graham's Motel
RT 219
Buckeye, WV 24924
(304) 799-4291

Greenbrier River Trail
c/o Watoga State Park
HC 82, Box 252
Marlinton, WV 24954-9550
(304) 799-4087

Jack Horner's Corner Convenience Store
HC 64 Box 521
Seebert, WV 24946
(304) 653-4515

Lewisburg Visitors Center
Carnegie Hall - 105 Church Street
Lewisburg, WV 24901
(304) 645-1000
(800) 833-2068

McNeill's Country Mart Inc.
Route 219
Buckeye, WV 24924
(304) 799-6880

Old Clark Inn
702 Third Avenue
Marlinton, WV 24954
(304) 799-6377

Monongahela National Forest
Recreation Specialist
200 Sycamore Street
Elkins, WV 26241
(304) 636-1800

Monongahela National Forest
White Sulphur Springs Ranger District
410 East Main Street
White Sulphur Springs, WV 24986
(304) 536-2144

Monongahela National Forest
Marlinton Ranger District
P. O. Box 210
Marlinton, WV 24954-0210
(304) 799-4334

Moore's Lodge
Back Mountain, Rt. 1 (5 miles southwest of Cass)
Stony Bottom, WV 24927
(304) 456-4721

Pocahontas County Tourism Commission
P. O. Box 275
Marlinton, WV 24954
(304) 799-4636
(800) 336-7009

Pocahontas Memorial Hospital
RR 2, Box 52 W (on RT 219, 2 miles south of
    Marlinton)
Buckeye, WV 24924
(304) 799-7400

Randolph County Convention & Visitors Bureau
200 Executive Plaza
Elkins, WV 26241
(800) 422-3304

Seneca State Forest
Route 1, Box 140
Dunmore, WV 24934
(304) 799-6213

Silver Creek Resort
P. O. Box 83
Snowshoe, WV 26291
(800) 523-6329

Snowshoe Mountain Biking Center
P. O. Box 10
Snowshoe, WV 26209
(304) 572-1000

Stillwell Park
P. O. Box 415
Marlinton, WV 24954

USGS Map Distribution
Federal Center, Building 41
Box 25286
Denver, CO 80225

Woods, Waters, and Wheels
200 West Washington Street
Lewisburg, WV 24901
(304) 645-5200

Watoga State Park
HC 82, Box 252
Marlinton, WV 24954-9550
(304) 799-4087

West Virginia Department of Transportation
Division of Highways
Transportation Planning Division, Map Sales
1900 Kanawha Boulevard East, Building 5
Charleston, WV 25305-0430
(304) 558-2868

West Virginia Division of Tourism
2101 Washington Street East
Charleston, WV 25305-0312
(304) 558-2286
1-800-CALL-WVA

West Virginia Geological and Economic Survey
Mont Chateau Research Center
P. O. Box 879
Morgantown, WV 26507-0879
(304) 594-2331

West Virginia Rails to Trails Council
P. O. Box 8889
South Charleston, WV 25303
(304) 722-6558

West Virginia Scenic Trails Association
633 West Virginia Avenue
Morgantown, WV 26505

Yew Mountain Lodge
Lobelia Road
HCR 64 Box 277
Hillsboro, WV 24946
(304) 653-4821

Appendix II
Former Railroad Stops Along the West Fork Trail

The mileage and elevation figures given here are from the 1925 County Survey published by the West Virginia Geological Survey or estimates from maps or the field. The elevations provided may not correspond to the elevation of the right of way but to some nearby feature.

MILEPOST	STATION NAME	ELEVATION
(Miles from Baltimore)		

Randolph County

MILEPOST	STATION NAME	ELEVATION
274.70	Elkins	1933
293.50	Bemis	2591
295.5	Greenbrier Junction	
295.9	Red Roaring Run	
296.80	Morribell	2838
296.8	Cheat Junction	2840
298.8	Tunnel #2 Summit	2939
299.20	Glady	2915
302.0	Beulah	

Pocahontas County

MILEPOST	STATION NAME	ELEVATION
302.7	Summit Cut	3147
305.80	Wildell	3060
308.7	Gertrude	3006
310.60	May	2963
311.1	Benchmark at NE corner of the concrete abutment to the trestle	2965.7
313.90	Burner	2923
314.0	Benchmark at West end of South stone abutment on trestles over Little River	2916.7
316.10	Braucher	2882

319.6	Olive	
319.6	Benchmark at trestle over	
	Mountain Lick Creek	
	280 feet east of Olive	2785
321.80	Durbin	2723

APPENDIX III
Former Railroad Stops Along the Greenbrier River Trail

The names and milepost figures given here were provided by William Price McNeel. A number of stops were located in the same vicinity in different years, frequently using the same name. For more detail, I suggest Mr. McNeel's book, *The Durbin Route*. Elevation figures were taken from the Pocahontas County Survey (1929) and the West Virginia Gazetteer of Physical and Cultural Place Names (1986) published by the West Virginia Geological Survey. The elevations provided may not correspond to the elevation of the right of way but to some nearby feature.

MILEPOST	STATION NAME	ELEVATION
00.00	Whitcomb	1705
01.82	North Caldwell (Little Sulphur, Hunter)	1696
02.90	Brickyard (Stone House)	
03.54	Camp Allegheny (Tottens)	1740
05.55	Hopper (Harper, Harpers)	1760
07.29	Bowes	
08.71	Loopemount	1840
09.32	Brink	1840
11.09	Keister Station	1774
14.12	Anthony	1800
16.11	Woodman	1819
17.01	Deeter	
19.30	Gardner	1880
21.53	Spring Creek	1862
24.77	Renick	1877
26.27	DeHart	
28.19	Golden	1898.09

29.64	Horrock	1916
30.62	Rorer	1931
32.10	Droop Mountain	1943
36.02	Spice Run	1989.9
37.72	Locust (Breakneck)	1999.1
38.48	Beard (Beards)	2010
39.33	Denmar (Den Mar)	2015.8
40.89	Mill Run	2025.3
41.70	Burnsides	2028.8
42.47	Kennison (Rexrode)	2036
45.77	Seebert	2059.4
46.32	Warns	
48.10	Watoga	2079.8
49.24	Violet (Dan)	2085.8
50.32	Improvement Lick	2080
52.18	Buckeye	2107.2
53.92	Munday Lick (Monday Lick)	2200
55.06	Stillwell	2127.9
56.13	Marlinton	2127.4
59.36	Knapp	2155
60.25	August	2165.9
61.28	Thorny Creek	2174.6
62.40	Clawson (Harper)	2185.6
64.55	Harter	2210.6
65.86	Sharps Tunnel	
66.73	Big Run	2248.58
68	Lombardy	
70.11	Camper	
71.17	Cloverlick	2295
74.37	Stony Bottom	2329
76.79	Sittlington (Forrest)	2363.6
78.02	Moses Run	2383
78.46	Raywood	2392.3
79.55	Deer Creek	2417.2
80.68	Cass	2441.5

82.58	Cup Run	2460
84.40	Wanless	2508.6
87.01	Nida	2564.7
88.17	Hosterman (Collins)	2584.5
92.21	Boyer Station (Nottingham P.O.)	2661.7
95.55	Durbin	2724
96.48	Frank	2736
97.88	Bartow	2774.1
99	Houchins	
100.46	Thornwood (Dunlevie)	2871
100.72	Winterburn	2868

Appendix **IV**
Selected Place Names Along the Trails

Man has derived the names of natural and man-made features from many sources. This list is an attempt to identify the origin of some of the current and historical place names close to either The West Fork or Greenbrier River Trails. Like any such list, it is doomed to be incomplete from the beginning. Time passes and few people remember why a town or stream was given its name. Years after a family such as the Bowes have sold their land to the railroad and moved away, we can only conjecture that the railroad stop was named for them.

Many locations used more than one name. The reasons behind these changes are often lost in time. One reason for changing the name of a location along a railroad was to avoid confusion with another stop on the same or another rail system. Some names varied because of the broad range in education and spelling ability of those who used them. Others occurred by shortening names such as "Moses Spring Run" to "Moses Run". Still other changes occurred by dropping apostrophes in the possessive form. Apparently, this practice of dropping all apostrophes in the possessive form of names was always routine for the railroad and has become the standard practice in gazetteers.

This list is organized with the names of the counties first, then the rivers, then other place names from north to south along both trails.

Greenbrier County and River (Green Briar or Green Bryer) — An English translation of the French *ronce verte*. The French named the river for the common greenbrier (*Smilax rotundifolia*), also known as catbrier, sometime before 1749. After English settlers translated the river's name, they also used it for the county. Later a small town south of Lewisburg was named Ronceverte.

Pocahontas County — Named for Pocahontas, also known as Matoaka, the daughter of Chief Powhatan in early colonial Virginia. Reportedly this name means "he or she who plays" or "the merry-minded." This is an apt name for a region full of leisure time activities.

Randolph County — Named for Edmund Jennings Randolph, a jurist and the Governor of Virginia from 1786 to 1788.

Shavers Fork — Probably named for Paul Shaver (or Schaeffer) born in 1759. He entered the area about 1774.

Cheat River — Three options are available for the person trying to determine the origin of this name. Cheat was an inferior type of rye. When the settlers could not get a good crop to grow, they felt they had been sowing cheat instead of wheat. A second story is that it is a misspelling of the surname Cheak or Cheal. The third theory is that the name is based on the "deceptive waters." Either the depth of the water was deceiving or the volume of water was so variable that it was deceiving.

Bemis (Fishing Hawk) — The original name, Fishing Hawk, derives from Fishing Hawk Creek, on which the town is located. Fishing Hawk is another name for the osprey, a bird once common here. The current name was in honor of Mr. Harry Bemis, a lumber operator from the days of the Coal and Iron Railroad. J. M. Bemis and Son was the name of the lumber company located here.

Morribell — The Morribell Lumber Company operated here before 1920. This name came from the surnames

Morrison and Bell, the original operators of the mill here. This company later became Morrison, Shields, and Gross.

Glady (Glady Fork) — The town, the river, and the lumber company were named from the glades located along the Glady Fork of the Cheat River.

Wildell — This name was created from the names of the Wilson and the Diehl families, who owned the Wildell Lumber Company. An alternate origin involves Merritt Wilson and Delle Wilson, his wife. This company was organized in Cumberland, Maryland and operated here. Interestingly, there is one photograph showing a rail car with three "l's" in the town's name and four "l's" in the company name.

Gaudineer Scenic Area — Several places in the area are named for Don Gaudineer. He was a ranger in the Greenbrier District of the Monongahela National Forest. When fire threatened his family, he gave his life to save them.

Beulah — The Beulah Lumber Company operated here before 1920.

Burner — All the place names (mountain, settlement and the hamlet) are derived from the surname Burner. Abram (or Abraham) Burner is the earliest known Burner in this area, probably living here in the late 1790's or early 1800's.

Durbin — The connecting link between the C & O and the Western Maryland Railroad. The name is in honor of Mr. Charles R. Durbin, Sr. Mr. Durbin was the cashier at the Grafton bank, which loaned the money to Mr. John T. McGraw to buy the site about 1890.

Frank — Named for Frank Hoffman, a Wheeling businessman and member of the Pocahontas Tanning Company, which had a tannery here.

Bartow (Travellers Repose) — The current name was given about 1904 after Camp Bartow, which was a civil war camp located nearby. The military camp was named for a Colonel Bartow. A General F. S. Bartow was killed in the first battle of Bull Run, and may be the man it was named for. The earlier name was after a well-known hotel on the Staunton-Parkersburg Pike.

Leatherbark Run — Several other streams and places in West Virginia are named leatherbark. All, apparently, after the leatherbark or leatherwood shrub. Its distinctive coloring would make it stand out among the local pines. The twigs of this shrub were used by Indians and early settlers to tie up small packages because they were as flexible as leather. This stream is notable because it heads up within 1,060 feet of the headwaters of Shavers Fork. In a short time, (geologically speaking) it is expected to erode further into the mountain and "capture" the upper 2 miles of the Shavers Fork. These 2 miles of Shavers Fork will then flow south with the Greenbrier rather than north with the Cheat. The word "run" means a small stream, brook, or other natural water course. It can also be a seasonal channel or overflow.

Cass — Named in 1899 after Joseph Cass, Chairman of the Board of the West Virginia Pulp and Paper Company.

Raywood — This area was once owned by a family named Ray.

Moses Run or Moses Spring Run — Moses Spring Run was a stream just to the west of this station. Moses

Moore was an early settler in the county. The stream was named for a spring, which in turn was named for him. He was camped near this spring when he was captured by five or six Indians "on the Sabbath," sometime between 1770 and 1786. He was forced to march with the Indians to Chillicothe. He later escaped and made his way back home. When the station took its name from the stream, "Spring" was dropped from it.

Sitlington (Forrest) — The name was changed from Forrest to Sitlington in 1904. It was named for Sitlington Creek, which enters the Greenbrier River opposite the trail. The stream was, in turn, named for Robert Sitlington, an early settler in the area who later moved to Dunmore. One source records a family named Forrest living near here. Others believes that the original name came from Mr. Forrest Moore, not the surname.

Stony Bottom (Driftwood or Seldom Seen) — Named in 1902 by W. R. Moore because the level bottom land there was very rocky. Originally the area was called Driftwood or Seldom Seen because it was so isolated. Each postmaster seemed to choose his own name for this community.

Clover Lick — Named for a nearby farm established in pre-Revolutionary War days. The farm took its name from the fields of clover that surrounded a salt lick. Ligon was considered as the name for the railway stop here after Dr. John Ligon, the Postmaster. However, this name was never used.

Big Run — There are twenty-one streams named Big Run in West Virginia.

Lombardy — The name for this station, Lombardy, probably came from some of the many Italian laborers who built the railroad and logged the mountains in the area. Among those who settled here were the Anastasias, the Corsos, the Circostas, the Dominicis, and the Porteleses. Some members of these families moved to California during World War II. Upon the death of the patriarch of the clan, Patsy Anastasia, most of the rest followed.

Sharps Tunnel — Named for the property owner at the time the tunnel was built. Presumably this owner was one of the descendants of William Sharp, Jr., an early settler in the area. The William Sharp, Jr. Pioneer Cemetery is located nearby. The land is now owned by David Buddy Workman and his family.

Harter — William J. and Albert M. Harter operated The Harter Brother's Lumber Company mill on a spur here from 1903 to 1911.

Clawson — Named after Reverend Samuel Clawson. I have heard that the station was originally named Harper, from the right of way grantor. The potential confusion between a station named Harper in Pocahontas County and a crossing named Harpers in Greenbrier County explains why this name didn't stick. Edray, from the Biblical name Edrai, was considered for this station but it was never used.

August — Mr. J. A. August, Jr., Mr. R. T. August and Mr. R. Q. Young operated a circular mill across the river from 1899 to 1901. They are credited with shipping the first load of lumber on the new railroad. The mill operated until 1910, though August and Young sold out in 1901.

Knapp — Possibly named for the nearby stream. Its

alternate name, Sixty, was derived from the nearby milepost on the railroad.

Marlinton (Marlins Bottom) — Both names are derived from Jacob Marlin who settled here in 1749. He was the first recorded settler west of the Allegheny Mountains in present day West Virginia.

Knapps Creek (Ewings Creek) — The original name, Ewings Creek, was after Captain James Ewing, an early settler and soldier in the Revolutionary War. He died about 1800. It was later changed to Naps (or Knapps) Creek after Napthalim Gregory, who is alleged to have been killed near here by outlaws about 1750. Whatever the exact circumstances, he disappeared "suddenly and mysteriously." However, between 1750 and 1752 a plot of land was surveyed in the sinks area of Monroe County for Nap or Knapp Gregory, along with a separate one for James Ewing. Gregory's report on this area led Jacob Marlin and Sewell to settle here.

Sunday Lick Run — Just to the north of Monday Lick Run, this name refers to an incident in which a deer was illegally killed at a salt lick on a Sunday. The name was intended to serve as a perpetual embarrassment to the poacher.

Monday Lick Run — The stream got its name from Len Monday, a pioneer hunter who roamed the area.

Munday Lick — Named after Monday Lick Run, a nearby stream. The variation in spelling is typical.

Buckeye (Buckeye Cove or Swago) — Reputedly called Buckeye or Buckeye Cove because John and James Bridger were killed by Indians under a buckeye tree in 1786. This was the last Indian raid in the county. It is more likely that the name is simply for the trees that grow plentifully in the area. A cove is a sheltered recess in the mountains such as a hollow or dell. This area was also called Swago, after a nearby stream, which appears to be a variation of Oswego, a Seneca word that means "small water flowing into that which is large."

Improvement Lick Run — A lick is a deposit of salt left behind when a salt spring evaporates. It is called a lick because deer and other animals lick such a spot for its salt. Apparently, someone improved on the lick Mother Nature placed here.

Violet (Dan or Beaver Creek) — The current name probably comes from the small flower that is common in this area. The former name, Dan, was in honor of Dan O'Connell, a white pine lumberman. It may have been changed due to a stop called Dan on the railroad in McDowell County. Prior to 1901, this station was called Beaver Creek, after the nearby stream.

Watoga — A variation of the Cherokee word Watauga, which means "river of islands." Several places with the second spelling are located in the Carolinas. A number of African Americans traveled up from the Carolinas and worked in constructing the railroad. It is possible they brought the name with them.

Stevens Hole Run — Stephens Hole is a cave just north of Millpoint where Stephen Sewell once wintered in 1750. This stream originates at the cave.

Stamping Creek — According to Calvin Price, buffalo gathered along this stream would stamp their feet to chase away flies. Robert E. Lee and his troops camped along this stream during the Civil War.

Warns — The Warn Lumber Company owned and ran several mills and lumber operations in the area. The company took its name from Preston S. Warn, who was a major promoter of the company.

Seebert — After Jacob Seybert or Frederick Sybert, early residents of the area. A Lanty S. Seebert from Pocahontas County served in Company I, 25th Regiment of the Virginia Infantry, C. S. V. during the War Between the States. Obviously, the name has had several spellings through the years.

Kennison — Named after Charles and Jacob Kennison, who were early settlers and owners of the first whipsaw in the area. This name is sometimes spelled Kinnison. The nearby mountain is also spelled Kinnison.

Burnsides — After James Burnside, an early settler.

Denmar (Den Mar) — Named in 1910 by Mr. John A. Dennison, President of the Maryland Lumber Company.

Beard — Named for Josiah Beard, who built and operated a saw and grist mill near the mouth of Locust Creek about 1800.

Locust (Breakneck) — A nearby stream is called Locust Creek. The former name is derived from an incident where a cow fell off a cliff and broke its neck.

Spice Run — The station and the Spice Run Lumber Company, took their names from the stream. Both are derived from the North American shrub, spicewood or spicebush, (Lindera benzoin) also known as "Benjamin Bush." The leaves of this shrub were used to make tea, while the oily berries were used as a substitute for allspice. The bush is in the laurel family.

Droop Mountain — A railroad station, a stream and a mountain. So named because one end of the mountain seemed to droop into the Big Levels of Greenbrier County. At times it was called Drooping Mountain.

Rorer — This name was a common surname in western Virginia and West Virginia at the turn of the century.

Horrock — Horrocks Desk Company operated from 1904 until 1924 at Renick. A stub siding to serve this company was located here until 1935.

Golden — After Paul Golden, who located a sawmill here in 1917.

Renick (Falling Spring) — Although the town's name is Falling Spring, the official name of the post office is Renick. The town's name arose because of the presence of springs that have a gentle fall into the Greenbrier River. The latter name is for William Renick, who acquired land here in 1768.

Spring Creek — Named after the nearby stream that flows from a large spring to the northwest.

Garner Run — Gardener is a local community located on Garner Run. Both are named after the same local family.

Deeter — Named after the Kendall–Deeter Lumber Company located here.

Anthony — Named for a stream which enters the river on the east bank. It, in turn, was named for John Anthony, a white man and Indian scout who hunted throughout this region. Once upon a time, while hunting in the area, Anthony was discovered by Indians. He ran into a cave surrounded by a nearly impenetrable thicket. Since it was getting dark, the Indians decided to camp outside and go in after him by the morning light. During the night Anthony cut his boots so he could wear them backwards, with the heel forward, and slipped away. The Indians apparently thought he had been joined by a friend. Instead, Anthony was well on his way to Fort Union some 20 miles away. A second story states that Anthony was an Indian who was friendly to the new settlers. He frequently warned them of attacks. When his tribe discovered what was going on, they began chasing him towards the settlements. He ran into the cave when he was about to be captured. At dark the Indians built a fire in front of the cave to wait until morning when they could shoot him at their leisure. When only one guard was left awake, Anthony rushed the Indians, firing the double-barreled shotgun given to him by an Englishman. As he raced to the creek, he cut his foot on a sharp rock. The large amount of blood he shed, on land and in the water, led the Indians to believe he had been mortally wounded from their shots. They abandoned the chase. Another account has local settlers coming to investigate the shooting, thus saving Anthony's life. The last variation sounds more likely to me. The cave lies near present day Camp Wood, a summer camp for the West Virginia University Department of Geology since 1937. This camp began as Camp Alvon, a Civilian Conservation Corps camp in 1934.

Dodson Branch – Dodson was a family surname. A branch is anything analogous to the branch of a tree. In this case, it refers to a small stream which is a tributary to a larger stream.

Kister (Kiester Station or Judyton Post Office or Keyster) — Both the post office and the name of the station are from family names. Although this location is called "Kister" on current highway maps, the railroad and trail guide spell it "Keister." "Keysters Mill" can be found on an 1887 map of Greenbrier County shown inside the back cover of *A History of Greenbrier County* by Otis Rice. A. Judy is shown as a resident just west of Kister on the same map. In *Hardesty's Greenbrier County*, a William Judy is listed as the son of David and Catharine (Kesler) Judy. Noah L. Keister was buried in Neal's Chapel Cemetery in nearby Vago in 1893.

Loopemount — A variation of the French meaning "wolf mountain." It also may have been derived from the river looping around a mountain here.

Bowes — Named for local residents. J. H. Bowes is the name on the right-of-way deed in this area. The station was named in 1903. Clarence A. Bowes (1882-1892) and Burl P. Bowes (1912-1913) are buried in the Neal's Chapel Cemetery in nearby Vago.

Hopper (Harper or Harpers) – On source says this station was named for H. W. Hopper, who had a side track built here in 1901. Other sources say it was named for John Thomas Harper, who owned 775 acres of land along Anthony Creek just across the river. He owned and operated the J. T. Harper & Sons store in White Sulphur Springs. The variations appear to be caused by either poor spelling or pronunciation of the name. The road that crosses here is still called Harper Road. The similarity between any of the various versions of this name and the original name for Clawson explains why that name was changed from Harper to Clawson.

Camp Allegheny (Tottens) — The original name was from the family of Thomas K. Totten who purchased the First Manse of the Old Stone Church on a bluff overlooking the Greenbrier River here in 1902. This dwelling is still standing along CR 38 a short distance from the southern end of the trail. The name was changed from Tottens to Camp Allegheny in 1940, after the summer youth camp located nearby. Allegheny has had several spellings through the years. It means either "eternity" or "eternal footprints" from the nearly year-round snow in its hidden hollows.

Howard Creek — Enters the Greenbrier River at Caldwell and was named for John and Josiah Howard who toured the area with Peter Salley in 1742. Forty-two miles south of here another Howard Creek enters the Greenbrier River.

North Caldwell (Hunter or Little Sulphur) — The exact origin of the name Little Sulphur is lost in time, but is undoubtedly connected to the numerous sulphur springs in the area. In 1901 the depot was completed and named Hunter, in honor of John A. Hunter, one of the members of the Greenbrier River Boom, Lumber, Iron, Land, and Manufacturing Company. Carter B. Hunter, M. C. Hunter, and Frank R. Hunter were grantors for the right of way in this area. The town of Caldwell, located directly across the Greenbrier, was named for James R. Caldwell, another member of the Greenbrier River Boom, Lumber, Iron, Land, and Manufacturing Company. Due to confusion with a stop on the Norfolk and Western Railway, the name was changed in 1902 from Hunter to North Caldwell.

An Annotated Bibliography

Blackhurst, Warren E. *Your Train Ride Through History*, Parsons, WV: McClain Printing Co., Fourth Printing, 1983.

This small pamphlet is available at the Cass Depot and gives some basic information on the natural history and timbering in the area. Mr. Blackhurst also wrote a number of fictional and semi-fictional accounts of life in Cass, which are available at the Depot.

Bridge, Raymond. *Bike Touring: The Sierra Club Guide to Outings on Wheels*, San Francisco: Sierra Club, 1979.

Like most books published by the Sierra Club, this one is excellent.

Brooks, Maurice. *The Appalachians*, Boston: Houghton Mifflin Company, 1965.

An excellent overview of the entire Appalachian range from Canada to Georgia. Any visitor to the eastern mountains should read this volume.

Clarkson, Roy B. *On Beyond the Leatherbark: The Cass Saga*, Parsons, WV: McClain Printing Co., 1990.

Clarkson, Roy B. *Tumult on the Mountains: Lumbering in West Virginia 1770-1920*, Parsons, WV: McClain Printing Co., Eighth Printing, 1988.

These two books are excellent studies of the early days of the timber industry in Cass and West Virginia. The photographs alone are worth the price of these books.

De Hart, Allen. *Hiking the Mountain State: The Trails of West Virginia*, Boston: Appalachian Mountain Club, 1986.

As close to a definitive list of the trails in West Virginia as I have seen. Some items may change slightly or grow out-of-date with time, but overall it is very useful.

De Hart, Allen and Bruce Sundquist. *Monongahela National Forest Hiking Guide*, Charleston, WV: West Virginia Highlands Conservancy, Sixth Edition, 1993.

The most comprehensive listing of hikes in the Monongahela National Forest.

Fletcher, Colin. *The Complete Walker III*, New York: Alfred A. Knopf, Third Edition, 1984.

Like his earlier editions, this is an easy to read book on backpacking. This one text has all the "how to" information you need. All of Colin Fletcher's books are worth reading.

Hutchins, Frank. *Mountain Biking in West Virginia*, Charleston, WV: Quarrier Press, 1995.

The first book dedicated solely to taming the Mountain State with two wheels and a water bottle. Covers trails from seventeen parts of the state, with excellent maps and information on camping, lodging, and some local history.

Kenny, Hamill. *West Virginia Place Names*, Piedmont: The Place Name Press, 1945.

This is the definitive reference book for anyone intrigued with why we call places the names we do. Of course, not every place name can be found in it, but it is an excellent resource.

McNeel, William Price. *The Durbin Route: The Greenbrier Division of the Chesapeake & Ohio Railway*, Charleston, WV: Pictorial Histories Publishing Company, Second Printing, 1986.

The only history of the C & O rail line up the Greenbrier River.

McNeel, William Price. *The Greenbrier River Trail: Through the Eyes of History*, Charleston, WV: Pictorial Histories Publishing Company, 1997.

A guide to the railroad era along the Greenbrier River Trail.

Willis, Gil and Mary. *Mountain Bike Rides in Pocahontas County West Virginia*, Lewisburg, WV: Roadrunner Press, 1989.

A small book that lists a dozen rides around Pocahontas County.

About the Author

Jim Hudson has resided in the Kanawha River Valley of West Virginia for most of his life. During his early years, he and his family made numerous trips to both his mother's childhood home in Bartow, Pocahontas County, and to a family-owned camp near Anthony, Greenbrier County. This camp was beside the railroad that would later became the Greenbrier River Trail.

After years of hiking, canoeing, and camping in the Mountain State, Jim was introduced to mountain biking by his friend, Bill Robinson. Together the two have hiked and biked most of the rail trails in West Virginia, as well as many other trails in Virginia and West Virginia.

Jim has held several positions in state government. Currently, he is an Environmental Resources Specialist for the Division of Environmental Protection, Office of Water Resources. Jim received both his Bachelor of Arts degree in Geography, and his Master of Science degree in Safety Studies, from West Virginia University in Morgantown, West Virginia.

About the West Virginia Rails-to-Trails Council

Founded in 1991, the West Virginia Rails-to-Trails Council (WVRTC) is a statewide non-profit charity whose membership includes local rail trail foundations, enthusiasts, civic organizations, trail user groups, and businesses. Our work with the National Park Service in the New River Gorge has won the national Trails for Tomorrow award sponsored by DuPont and the American Hiking Society.

Our purpose is to promote and help create rail trails in West Virginia to provide recreational opportunities and stimulate economic development through rail trail tourism.

The West Virginia Rails-to-Trails Council carries out a program of:

- Public education and information
- Local rail trail project support and statewide advocacy
- Volunteer support to assist rail trail development and maintenance.

West Virginia Rails-to-Trails Council
MEMBERSHIP APPLICATION

[ ] YES, I am interested in helping to convert
abandoned railroad corridors into public trails.

[ ] I want to become a member of the West Virginia
Rails-to-Trails Council (check dues level):

[ ] $10.00 Individual
[ ] $25.00 Family
[ ] $50.00 Small Business
[ ] $100.00 Trail Builder
[ ] $100.00 Organization (voting)
[ ] Other $_____

Please make your check payable to:

West Virginia Rails-to-Trails Council
P. O. Box 8889
South Charleston, WV 25303

Name
_____

Address
_____

City, State, Zip
_____

Phone (W)   (H)
_____

[ ] Yes, send me the Adventure Guide to WV Rail Trails
for $7.95 plus $2.00 shipping.